QUESTIONS AND ANSWERS

on the

SCIENCE OF MIND

Other books by Ernest Holmes

CREATIVE MIND

CREATIVE MIND AND SUCCESS

THE SCIENCE OF MIND

HOW TO USE THE SCIENCE OF MIND

THIS THING CALLED LIFE

THIS THING CALLED YOU

WORDS THAT HEAL TODAY

QUESTIONS AND ANSWERS

on the

SCIENCE OF MIND

ERNEST HOLMES

AND

ALBERTA SMITH

Science of Mind Publications
Los Angeles, California

Science of Mind Publications Edition
Second Printing — March 1983

Originally published by Dodd, Mead & Company, New York
Copyright © 1935, 1963 by Institute of Religious Science

Printed in the United States of America
ISBN: 0-911336-88-5
Cover Design: Robert R. Tompkins

SCIENCE OF MIND PUBLICATIONS
3251 W. Sixth Street—P.O. Box 75127
Los Angeles, California 90075

FOREWORD TO THE
SCIENCE OF MIND PUBLICATIONS EDITION

The Science of Mind philosophy has been helping people for over fifty years. Developed by the American metaphysician Ernest Holmes (1887–1960), this spiritual approach to personal well-being has aided countless thousands of persons in their search for a more fulfilling life.

A number of books have been written which amplify the teachings of Dr. Holmes, and *Questions and Answers on the Science of Mind* is outstanding among them. Co-authored by Alberta Smith—a graduate of the first Practitioner class ever taught by Ernest Holmes—it specifically addresses hundreds of commonly asked questions about the Science of Mind viewpoint, as well as conveying to the reader a *feeling* for the inspiration which is central to this powerful philosophy.

Science of Mind Publications is pleased to present *Questions and Answers* to a new generation of readers, knowing that the practical application of spiritual principles—though a timeless art—deserves attention today even more than it did nearly five decades ago when this book was first published.

FOREWORD TO THE FIRST EDITION

The Institute of Religious Science is happy to present this new and enlarged edition of *Questions and Answers on the Science of Mind*. The questions in this book have been asked over a period of many years through the medium of the *Science of Mind* Magazine and local classwork. Therefore, we feel these questions and answers will meet a real need.

Great credit is given to Irene Haughey, through whose labor of love and intelligence several thousand questions were classified, and from them the most significant selected.

CONTENTS

PART I
The Nature of Being

PART II
The Nature of Mankind

PART III
Spiritual Healing

PART IV
Authority Over Conditions

PART V
Miscellaneous Questions and Answers

QUESTIONS AND ANSWERS

on the

SCIENCE OF MIND

PART I

The Nature of Being

MEANING OF DIVINE MIND

Question—Why do we say Universal Intelligence, Divine Mind, etc., and why do we use other names in place of God when all mean the same? This is confusing to a beginner.

ANSWER—When we say conscious life, spirit, conscious mind, objective mind, Christ Mind, self-conscious mind, we always mean the same thing: that thing. in a person which enables him to be consciously aware of himself. When we say subjective, subconscious, creative consciousness, creative mind, soul, unconscious, psyche, we mean that thing in a person which automatically reacts to his conscious thought. When we use the same words in relation to the Infinite Being we mean the same thing on the scale of the Universal.

THE SPIRIT OF MAN

Question—What is the spirit of man since it cannot be seen?

ANSWER—We do not see beauty, we see that which is beautiful. We do not see love, we see that which is lovely. We feel the presence of love through loveliness as we sense an atmosphere of beauty in that which is beautiful. We do not see intelligence but we see its manifestation. "No man has seen God at any time, only the son he has revealed him," means that we do not see the First Cause, but the effect which is the result of this First Cause is a positive evidence of the reality of its Cause.

WHO MAY USE THE LAW

Question—Can the same results be obtained by anyone using the law of mind and Spirit without any previous knowledge of this law?

ANSWER—Most certainly. The law of mind and Spirit is a universal law and we are all using it every moment.

INVOLUTION AND EVOLUTION EXPLAINED

Question—What do we mean by involution and evolution?

ANSWER—Before anything can evolve it must first be involved. Before the seed can produce a harvest it must fall into the ground. The planting of the seed is involution, an invoking of the law of productivity. The seed is an idea specializing the law, having a definite purpose, that of producing its own type. The act of involution is a conscious one. The gardener consciously invokes the law. As soon as the seed is planted, the natural processes of creation begin. Everything that happens from seed to harvest is intelligent but unconscious, hence a mechanical process. When we study evolution we are studying a mechanism and not a spontaneity. Involution precedes evolution in the creative sequence. Evolution follows involution with a mechanical exactness.

THE INFINITE

Question—Is the Infinite neither increased nor decreased by the existence or the non-existence of other realities to which It gives their derived being?

ANSWER—The Infinite is neither increased nor decreased because that to which It gives a derived being is still the Infinite manifesting Itself from Its own self-existence.

SELF-KNOWINGNESS OF SPIRIT

Question—What is meant by the Self-knowingness of Spirit?

ANSWER—By the Self-knowingness of Spirit we mean that

God, or First Cause, or Principle, is conscious of Its own Being. It is, and It knows. It knows Itself to be Absolute, All. It knows Itself to be Life, Idea and Manifestation. It knows Itself to be Free Choice and Volition. It knows that there is nothing outside of Itself. It is conscious of Itself as All there is. It knows Itself to be Truth, Love, Cause and Effect. Spirit is the only Power in the Universe that is conscious of Itself, or of Its Beingness.

SPIRIT—SELF-KNOWINGNESS

Question—How may we develop spiritual insight?

ANSWER—Emerson said, "We must learn to listen greatly to the self." One should practice being perfectly still and waiting for one's own mind to speak. One should listen, not as though he were making himself receptive to spirit influences, but knowing that perfect Intelligence flows through him. For instance, if one desires to know anything relative to a certain proposition, he should seek to know that the Infinite Intelligence operating through him acquaints him with the answer to his problem. Thus God's knowledge becomes our conscious knowledge. Wisdom passes from potentiality into actuality.

INTELLIGENCE AND EVOLUTION

Question—Is intelligence the result of evolution?

ANSWER—No. Evolution is the result of intelligence. The starting point of evolution *is* intelligence, the unfolding of intelligence *is* evolution.

GOD AND THE LAW

Question—Is the term Divine Law used by Religious Scientists synonymous with Mind or with God?

ANSWER—The term Divine Law is synonymous with the Universal Subjective Law. God as Spirit is synonymous with universal Intelligence in a conscious state, while Divine Law is subjective, and is never consciously conscious. It is never self-knowing but It is always self-doing. It knows how to do, but not what It is doing. The soil knows how to grow corn, but not that it is growing corn.

THE ANSWER TO OUR DESIRES

Question—What is it that answers definite desires and gives specific directions?

ANSWER—It is that in us which is one with the Spirit, wherein the potential of all knowledge exists, ready to spring into being. From this viewpoint there is no real question which does not have its answer in Mind. It is not necessarily conscious at the present time but it is potentially conscious and the moment a demand is made upon Mind the answer to this demand is created out of pure intelligence.

NO ULTIMATE, DESTRUCTIVE UNIVERSAL ELEMENT

Question—Is there a destructive element in the universe?

ANSWER—Forms are built up and disappear so that better ones may take their place in the scheme of evolution. Disregarding the apparent confusion, there is a stern and inescapable preference on the part of the universe, an inevitability of good; it will finally win. If the universe had actual destructive elements in it, it would be self-destroyed. "A kingdom divided against itself cannot stand."

ATTRIBUTES OF MIND

Question—What is meant by "in Mind." What Mind, whose Mind and where is this Mind?

ANSWER—The expression "in Mind" refers either to conscious Mind or Spirit, or to the universal principle which is subjective to Spirit. Mind is a dual unity. As Spirit it is conscious; as law it is subjective. The expression, "involved" or "implanted" in Mind, when one has given a treatment, means that the idea which he needs to know is now known in Mind and will be made known to him. Pure Spirit, which is the potential knowledge of everything, will now know directly through his individual use of It.

CREATIVE POWER OF MIND

Question—What is creative mind?

ANSWER—No one knows, any more than anyone knows what life is. Creative mind was never created. It must be co-existent and co-eternal with Spirit. It is a phase of Spirit. It is a law of intelligence executing the will of Spirit. It is an infinite medium surrounding us and flowing through us. Subject to our thought, it exists everywhere. It is available at all times, always responding by corresponding.

CONSCIENCE DEFINED

Question—What is a good definition of conscience?

ANSWER—It is a sense, an intuitive perception that there are certain things that work out right in the long run. If we wish, we can interpret it as being the voice of God. There is only One Voice in the Universe, which is the voice of God. We all may use this voice.

CREATIVE SUBJECTIVITY

Question—What is the nature of the Universal Subjective Mind?

ANSWER—Its nature is to be subjective and creative, sub-conscious but not unconscious, reacting intelligently, knowing how to react but having no self-determination. And the more clearly we keep this in mind, the more we shall see that it has no intention of its own, so far as we as individuals are concerned. We are now speaking of the Creative Law and not of the Universal Spirit. We must draw a very careful distinction between the two aspects of Reality.

THOUGHT AND FORM

Question—Upon what do thoughts act to produce form?

ANSWER—Upon the Universal Subjectivity, the Creative Medium. Form is an effect. The sequence of cause and effect is first pure intelligence, next an inner movement of pure intelligence by idea, then the movement of idea upon substance, next the passing of substance into form. In this sequence the only self-conscious movement is at the beginning; everything else is automatic; everything else is an effect. Even the idea is an effect of the intelligence which creates it. The form is a result of this idea. The starting point of all creation is in pure intelligence.

THOUGHT IS CREATIVE

Question—Explain why thought has creative power.

ANSWER—Thought has creative power because it is its nature to have it. It is impossible to decide why this is so. All that we can explain is how it works, insofar as our present knowledge enables us to understand how it works.

IS GOD PERSONAL?

Question—Does the metaphysician believe in a personal God?

ANSWER—He believes that God is the Life Principle through which man is identified as an intelligent self-choosing entity; that the mind in man is the Mind of God, since in unity there must and can be but the *One Mind*. The particular current of this One Mind which man uses habitually to serve his own personal needs, makes this Divine Mind or Intelligence very personal to him, as according to his choice and use, are his experiences. God, or Life Principle, therefore, is very personal to the individual. There comes to him a deep sense of inner communion, a spontaneous sense of irresistible union.

The metaphysician, therefore, sees and *feels* with clarity the truth about God and man.

MIND AND MATTER

Question—Does the Universal Subjectivity contain matter in the same way that conscious mind contains idea?

ANSWER—As Spirit is the potential source of all inspiration and all ideas that are ever to be expressed, so the Universal Subjectivity must be a potential of all the forms which are ever to evolve. Of itself it is an immaterial, unthinking, indeterminate stuff, having no desire of its own, being nothing of itself, yet being ever ready to take form.

NEUTRALIZING CONDITIONS BY DENIAL

Question—Will a positive denial of an existing condition neutralize the thought that caused this condition?

ANSWER—It will if one believes in the truth of his denial; if the mind is able to convince itself that negation has no true law to support it, no government of reality behind it.

TECHNIQUE OF THE SILENCE

Question—"Going into the Silence" is something I do not quite understand. Will you kindly explain?

ANSWER—The procedure called "Going into the Silence" is as follows: Sit comfortably in a chair in an alert attitude of mind. You are going into prayer, for a very definite purpose. The purpose of this particular silence should now be contemplated. If you seek health, the contemplation should revolve about the spiritual truth that in Divine Mind, where you are known by your own name, there is no connection between you and ill health. This thought should be dwelt upon and amplified until you have convinced your mind that illness is no part of the Divine Plan for your experience. Then you should unify your mind with the Divine Plan for your perfect health by gratefully determining to give up the habit of thinking illness, and resolve to think the truth about yourself.

Now say: "There is but the One Perfect Eternal Life and that life is my life. Perfect health is now established in me and in my mind. Perfect health is the law of my being, and from now on it shall be my conscious experience. I know the Law accepts my word and delivers to me the conscious manifestation of health, and I thank the great Spirit of Life for this fulfillment."

As you thus meditate, you are directing Mind and setting into motion the Divine Law. Your demonstration will be in the same degree as your belief. "Be still—and know." Know that you are answered before you call, just as surely as the light will shine in your face whenever you turn your face to the light.

This is an example of going into the Silence.

PERSONALNESS OF GOD

Question—Explain how one makes the concept of God personal, especially in connection with prayer. Law is such a cold thing.

ANSWER—When we desert the old idea of God, we have lost something, because we had a God to whom we could go, who we felt could hear and answer; when we think of a government of law we no longer have any Spirit to pray to and we are thrown into a spiritual abyss. But we pass through this state to the realization that we could not be conscious beings unless there were a First-consciousness in the universe. We could not be personified unless there were an Infinite Personalness. So we begin to see that there is an Infinite Personalness in the universe, an Infinite Presence (not an infinite person), the abstract and universal cause of all personalities. Then it begins to dawn upon us that where our life is personified, God is personified. So we regain the old idea of a personal God but with a less limited sense. "Who made the eyes, shall He not see. Who made the ears, shall He not hear. Who made the understanding, shall He not understand?" The personal God returns to us and is in us. Prayer becomes a communion and not a petition. The wave dips up from the ocean of Infinity and personifies itself through all people; hence, it is personal to all who understand its inner presence.

CONSCIOUSNESS AND MATTER

Question—What is the difference between consciousness and matter?

ANSWER—Consciousness has self-determination. Matter has none. It is the difference between the potter and the clay.

GOD NEVER TESTS US

Question—Does God test us to see if we are fit to enter the kingdom of heaven?

ANSWER—The kingdom of heaven is the place within ourselves where there is universal and individual peace at all times; peace that holds no element of doubt of one's abiding good and Divine, wise protection. To enter such a place, all that is necessary is to recognize that it exists exactly where Jesus taught us to seek it—within ourselves. We cannot contemplate such a place very long without taking on all the blessed attributes of its divinity, and we become Peace Itself.

God never tests us to see if we are fit for anything. God, within us, knows exactly what we are, which is nothing less than individualized centers of Himself. Man, having mental freedom, chooses to test himself sometimes, and finds himself wanting. That is, he discovers lack in his understanding. For if he had not the lack, he would never fail of his demonstration.

Sickness, inharmonies of many kinds, are often considered

as tests of the great loving God, but such is never the case. God knows nothing of tests. God knows only Perfect Being. Perfect Being is Peace, the kingdom of heaven. When we can contact that place within our consciousness, we are in the kingdom.

WHY WE BELIEVE

Question—What is it that makes us believe?

ANSWER—It is the Thing Itself announcing Itself through us. It is an intuitive perception, it is the Mind of God. It is the omnipresence of the universe, the self-assertion of Spirit that makes us believe.

THE INDIVIDUAL'S USE OF MIND

Question—What effect has the individual's thinking in this Universal Mind?

ANSWER—The individual's thinking in this Mind causes It to impersonate Itself through him at the level of his belief. It is by a law of reflection that this takes place—a response which corresponds, as a reflection in a mirror. This is known as the reciprocal action between the individual and the Universal.

WORDS "JESUS" AND "CHRIST" EXPLAINED

Question—What is the difference between Jesus and Christ?

ANSWER—Jesus is the name of a man. Christ means the Universal Principle of Divine Sonship—the generic man— the Divine Pattern—the ideal toward which humanity evolves —the apex of individual evolution—the conscious union of man with God. Jesus was the Christ. Jesus became increasingly the Christ as his mentality increasingly perceived the relationship of the man Jesus to the Christ principle, which is inherent in all people. This Christ has come in certain measures of power throughout the ages to different ones and still does come and is ever inherent within each of us.

"LAW OF CORRESPONDENCE" DEFINED

Question—What is meant by the "law of correspondence"?

ANSWER—By the "law of correspondence" is meant that there must be a subjective correspondence for every objective fact. The cause of all objective things exists in the field of subjectivity and for everything which transpires in the objective world there is an exact corresponding cause in the mental or spiritual world. This world responds by corresponding, through a law of reflection inherent within itself.

HOW INVISIBLE BECOMES VISIBLE

Question—You stated that when an individual's prayers are answered "that the invisible becomes visible." Please explain just how the invisible can become visible.

ANSWER—Creation is eternally going on. Prayer sets an invisible power in motion. This invisible power, which is Spirit, becomes form when there is a definite nucleus of thought around which it may take form. If you go into a garden you will see the invisible becoming visible, daily. The seed is the impulse, the law does the rest. So it is with thought.

MANIFESTING THE POTENTIAL BEING

Question—Explain the difference between a becoming God and an unfolding Infinite.

ANSWER—God is not becoming, by reason of the fact that there is nothing for the Infinite to change into but Itself. An unfolding Infinite means a continuous and a progressive manifestation of that which already is potential in Reality. First we have God, or Being, and as the complement of that which is First Cause, we have a becoming, a manifestation, or a creation which is eternally going on. "Becoming" is a progressive series of unfoldment. It is the passing of Spirit into form as the result of Its own instinctive and necessary self-contemplation.

SPIRIT AND MATTER

Question—What is the difference between matter and Spirit?

ANSWER—One is substance and the other is form. They are the same thing. Spirit takes form and that form is what we call matter.

FATHERHOOD OF GOD

Question—Does Religious Science teach that nothing exists but Mind, and that God is the Only Mind? If so, then if God is all, He has no children. Does this not strip the universe of the doctrine of divine love and the Fatherhood and Motherhood of God?

ANSWER—Religious Science teaches that there is one universal, self-consciousness or Spirit, which we call God; that there is a universal reaction to that spiritual consciousness, which is the law of mind in action, and that there is a universal manifestation, the result of the action of Spirit through law, which universal manifestation is called creation. To each individual this universal Spirit, which is the parent mind, is Father of all, and being personified through the individual, must, through his own nature, be immediately accessible to him.

CAN GOD KNOW EVIL?

Question—You said in a radio talk that God did not know evil. I have always been told that God knew everything. How about it?

ANSWER—God can only know that which is God, and if evil is God, then God can know evil. If evil is not God then God cannot know evil. As hate disappears when love dominates, as the darkness has no power over the light, as even hell is cooled by the breath of Heaven, so the devil cannot fight God. When "the eye views the world as one vast plane and one boundless reach of sky," the lesser irregularities disappear, so our troubles flatten when we gain the higher perspective of reality. Let those who feel so inclined argue over the problem of evil, but see to it that in your own mind you are the offspring of good alone and you will have solved the riddle of the universe.

REALITY TO FACT

Question—Please explain the difference between a fact and a reality.

ANSWER—Back of all actuality, or fact, is reality, out of which the form and action come. The actuality of God's nature is the fact of His expression in His creation. Reality corresponds to the Abstract, the Great Potential out of which all form emerges. The concrete is the objective universe with all its activities and forms.

The life at the center of all created things is the reality of those things, but the thing is the evidence of that life's presence—the thing is the fact. Reality and spiritual fact are not synonymous terms because the spiritual fact is held in solution, as it were, suspended within the Great Unformed Reality. Its projection sets it whirling in the universe of form, and we call it a fact. All facts have form, but "back of the apparent *is* the Reality."

FAITH IN TREATMENT

Question—How can I bring myself to the point of being able to give a good spiritual treatment when I doubt my ability to give a treatment because I do not seem to have faith enough in myself?

ANSWER—What is it you need to have faith in—yourself, your treatment, or the principle which you seek to demonstrate? How can you fail to give a good treatment when you understand that the power of a treatment lies in the fact that you are surrounded by a universal principle which executes the treatment? The only faith you need to have in yourself is the realization that the treatment is given according to law. The faith, then, is not in yourself, but in the law. "Be still and know that I am God."

PUNISHMENT FOR WRONG-DOING

Question—Do you teach there is no evil? For instance, is there no punishment for one who breaks the law?

ANSWER—Heaven is harmony and is a state of spiritual consciousness, while evil is a belief in a power opposed to God, the Good. Man makes his own heaven or his own hell right here and now. Evil is sometimes thought to be a very real thing but it has no vitality, no life, because it can always be destroyed by Truth. Change the mental concept and know that whatever constructive condition you vision, the same you actualize. You are the *all* Conquering Son of God. Accept love, harmony, happiness and peace and they will manifest in your life and indeed Heaven will be to you a radiant and illumined state of consciousness.

Yes, there is suffering for the lawbreaker, but it is not within your province or mine to condemn or judge our brother. Any so-called breaker of the law, spiritual or man-made, is sowing destructive seeds which must sooner or later return to him. This is according to law. It could not be otherwise, so let the law deal with him. Your work and mine toward our fellowman is not to condemn or judge harshly, but to see the perfect idea there, no matter how grievous the mistake. It is only in this way that the other condition can be neutralized.

LAW OF BELIEF

Question—How can one believe he has already received when all conditions contradict his belief?

ANSWER—He cannot, unless he first realizes that he is dealing with a law which takes his belief and produces a corresponding result.

LAW AN IMPERSONAL FORCE

Question—Is the Law of Mind an impersonal force?

ANSWER—In *The Science of Mind,* it is written: "Like all law, the Law of Mind is an Impersonal Force, and because of Its nature, is compelled to act."

The Law of Mind is impersonal yet everyone may consciously set It into activity to very definite and personal ends. One who realizes that his word is the mold which marks the form of his creation, who knows that the Law acts automatically upon this word, will speak or think only such words or thoughts as he would wish to see manifested. All mental and spiritual healers know how to use the Law of Mind to help themselves and others. They consciously direct their mental stream toward the desire they entertain, and know that it is a finished and perfect thing even as they think it. If they are speaking the healing word for some seeker after health, the realization of health which they hold for that person is acted out in the experience of the person by the Law of Mind. It has performed a very personal service, yet It is equally at the service and call of everyone.

SUBCONSCIOUS AND SUBJECTIVE

Question—What is the distinction between Subconscious and Subjective mind in metaphysical terminology?

ANSWER—There is no distinction. Each term means soul, or the receiving, automatic side of life. Subjective or subconscious mind receives the idea from Spirit, or the impress of our own thought, as a mold, and gives back to us the created thing, condition or circumstance which was formed by the mold. Subjective Mind is without the power of choice—it knows only to obey. It is not self-knowing. It is the Universal Medium and the Law by which all creation is produced.

HOW TO ACQUIRE CONVICTION

Question—How can a person be convinced of this law when he has not experienced a demonstration of it?

ANSWER—By intelligently and scientifically working until he does make a demonstration. He should take some simple problem and mentally treat it until he sees it objectify. Then he knows and has created a foundation upon which to build.

CONCENTRATION AND MEDITATION

Question—What is the difference between concentration and meditation?

ANSWER—From our viewpoint, concentration means to bring some definite thought to the conscious attention. It is self-evident that we do not need to concentrate Divine Energy since it is Omnipresent. What we do is to focus our conscious attention, and in this way permit Divine Energy to take the form of our desire. The degree of power focused will be according to our mental and spiritual equivalent. In other words, our power is equal to our faith in it.

For example, if you wish to concentrate on some particular thought, bring your attention to it then hold it, but without effort. At first you will find other thoughts coming in to interfere, but do not oppose them; brush them aside and resume your contemplation.

WHY DO WE THINK EVIL?

Question—If there is a Thinker behind all, who does the thinking, and if He is all good, why do we think evil?

ANSWER—There is but one Thinker and one Mind behind all. To think otherwise is to suppose duality, and duality cannot be.

That this One is the essence of Goodness is necessary, else the universe would be self-destructive. That this One is the Original Cause is certain, and that this Cause is a perfect Unit is self-evident.

Man exists in this One, but with perfect freedom, since he is an individual with the power of selection or choice, without which power there could be no real freedom. But man is on the pathway of unfoldment and does not yet fully comprehend his true nature. In ignorance of this nature he brings calamity upon himself through a *misuse* of the creative powers of his being.

In reality, God is the first Thinker, the true Cause. This Cause flows through man at the level of his comprehension of It. Man thinks limitation. The result which follows is not *real* limitation but an expression of his freedom, which freedom is so *complete* that it causes him to *appear* limited. *Man is bound by his freedom rather than by any real bondage.*

To believe only in the good is to demonstrate that the good *alone* has real power.

THE EVER-PRESENT GOD

Question—How can one picture an ever-present God in and through everything?

ANSWER—He sees in everything some manifestation of the Divine. He sees in every person some manifestation of the Christ. He sees a potential Divinity in all people.

MIRACLES AND FAITH

Question—Are so-called miracles just as demonstrable as ordinary events, if one has sufficient faith?

ANSWER—Yes, a miracle is merely something we are not

accustomed to seeing or experiencing. In reality there are no miracles, for what seems to be a miracle is but a supremely natural law. The faith that can bring about the least demonstration can bring about the greatest. Great and small exist only in the consciousness of man. In the Universal Mind there is but *one element*—completion or perfection. Whatever an individual can believe in his mind, can become objectified in his experience. Intellectually, he may know a thing for a long time but it will never be more than a mental thing to him until his intellectual knowing is corroborated by his spiritual feeling and conviction. Once this action has taken place, he is so imbued with the Truth about the thing that his certainty on the subject is bound to project itself into being. Many people demonstrate without consciously reasoning a thing out at all. Their intuitional capacity is greater, or rather more developed, than their intellectual capacity, and by following their hunches, they have proved to themselves that such leadings are trustworthy. Obedience to a true hunch will project into outer manifestation some certain experience, *but merely considering the thing from an intellectual point of view will never objectify any experience.*

DIVINE SELF-CONFIDENCE

Question—Define Divine self-confidence.

ANSWER—Divine self-confidence is a result of the knowledge that the self is governed, protected and sustained by the Spirit.

IS VISUALIZING HOLDING A THOUGHT?

Question—How can the statement that we should not hold thoughts be reconciled with the endeavor to visualize, or see, things mentally as we wish them to be? Is not the effort to visualize a thing as it should be, the act of "holding a thought"?

ANSWER—There is a difference between visualization and holding thoughts. To visualize means to mentally see, to conceive of an image in thought of some definite desire, while holding thoughts too often becomes a mere process of *willing* things to happen. It is not necessary either to hold thoughts or visualize in order to demonstrate—although visualization might often be a very substantial prop to the acquirement of a correct consciousness. As the plant is potential in the seed, so the thing inheres in the concept of it, and every word, as has been stated by a great thinker, carries its own mechanics with it. Thought should be loosed, not held, but loosed in the full conviction that it is a tangible, definite, spiritual entity in an intelligent and receptive law, whose business it is to take the concept and evolve it into tangible form.

MEANING OF THE DIVINE PLAN

Question—What is the Divine plan for each one of us?

ANSWER—The aim of evolution is to produce an individual who is conscious of himself, conscious of experience and increasingly conscious of his unity with the whole. Theoretically speaking, this would produce illimitable numbers of beings, each approximating the Infinite, but no one ever becoming the Infinite; all living in unity with It, in conscious oneness without division. This is the concept of concepts, the place that the illumined have reached.

HER LIFE MUST SHOW IT

Question—In a case in which the husband is very materialistic and the wife is interested in Religious Science, what should the wife do to win her husband over and enjoy harmony in the home life?

ANSWER—The wife should not try to "win her husband

over" to Religious Science or to anything else. He is an individual and so is she. Each should let the other alone to work out his own problem.

If, however, the wife is interested in the Truth and the husband is not interested and if the wife, without argument, will demonstrate that she really has something worthwhile, and if her life shows it, she will find that her husband will already be won over.

In the Truth, we never coerce or argue with anyone. Truth known is demonstrated and, demonstration being self-evident, it will be accepted by all.

Let the wife watch her own steps in Truth and if these steps lead to the altar of reality, the husband will follow gladly.

GREATEST HANDICAP TO SPIRITUAL PROGRESS

Question—What do you believe to be man's greatest handicap to spiritual progress?

ANSWER—A lack of belief in the actual presence of Spirit as directing and Law as obeying; the lack of a spontaneous acceptance of Good as being an absolute power over evil; the lack of a belief in the possibility of directly approaching a conscious intelligence through one's own mind and receiving a direct answer from it. Doubt, fear, uncertainty and a sense of isolation hinder the progress of this desirable mental attitude.

SEEKS SPIRITUAL UNFOLDMENT

Question—Above everything else I want spiritual unfoldment. I hear so many people say they would like to know God's universal law, but cannot know how to contact it or apply it or make it their own. Will you please give a simple, direct way in which beginners may understand the universal law, a direct way of applying it?

ANSWER—The first thing for beginners or those who are

not beginners to realize is that they are surrounded by intelligent Spirit operating through perfect law. Very few people have an adequate idea of the meaning of spiritual experience and fail to realize the simplicity of the application of the law. Learn to come to the Spirit *within you* as a child approaches its parents. Never try to use other people's words, but put your thoughts in your own words and approach reality directly in your own thought. That which the sages and the saints have known, you can know as well as they. Let nothing stand between you and It, and believe with all your mind that the Spirit is making Itself manifest to you.

SEPARATING BELIEF FROM BELIEVER

Question—How does one separate the belief from the believer?

ANSWER—He endeavors to understand what the belief is, either through his intuitive perception, through what the person tells him, or through his observation of the physical circumstances surrounding the person. Whatever is of a negative, destructive or unhappy nature he declares to be neither person, place, nor thing; therefore, it cannot operate in, around or through the person. First he turns the condition into a thought, then he separates the thought from the one thinking it.

ARE PRIMITIVE PEOPLE SPIRITUAL?

Question—Is there a beneficent law for the primitive races whose spiritual faculties are not developed and who can only function in the material aura of physical life?

ANSWER—There is one law common to all people and all races, and each according to his light is consciously or unconsciously using this law. Evolution is the result of the unfoldment of consciousness, and the law is always reacting to us at the level of our recognition of life. There is a tendency or an urge behind all things for expression. Through experience we learn to provide a larger outlet for this urge and thus both developed and undeveloped people continually progress with a limitless possibility ever before them. The law is always beneficent.

THE PERFECT UNIVERSE

Question—How does Religious Science account for the presence of a Universe which is perfect?

ANSWER—We must realize the Perfect Universe if we wish to embody the greatest good. If the Universe were not perfect it could not exist for a single moment. It is self-evident that we live in a Perfect Universe; and, if so, then everything in it must also be perfect.

The Truth is Indivisible and Whole. God is Complete and Perfect. A Perfect Cause must produce a Perfect Effect. Disregarding all evidence to the contrary, the student of Truth will maintain that he lives in a Perfect Universe and among perfect people; he will regulate his thinking to meet this necessity and will refuse to believe in its opposite. At first he may appear to be weak; but as time goes on, he will prove to himself that his position is a correct one, for that which appears imperfect will begin to slip from his experience.

PERSONAL CHOICE IS DIVINE FREEDOM

Question—What do you mean in Religious Science by being "free"?

ANSWER—Free Spirit means that which cannot be bound; It is free to do as It chooses, but cannot, of course, do anything that denies Its own nature. Freedom of will means the ability to do, say or think as one wishes; to express life as one personally desires. To be able only to think and dream of freedom would not be liberty. To imagine, without the power to manifest that imagination, would be to remain in a sort of dream world which would never come to complete self-realization. This is not the world in which man lives at all, for man's world is one of self-expression, even though that expression appears at times to destroy him.

Freedom, then, means to eliminate from consciousness all those things which bind and limit the free flowing of the Divine Spirit through man, and at the same time, exercising the faculty of personal choice. Keeping the personal choice immersed in the divine flow of Spirit—one with It—brings to us the power that Jesus used, and the works that he did become possible to us. Man binds himself only by thinking, and it is because his mind *is* the mind of God that his thought is effective. He automatically claims his freedom when he is convinced that he can use no mind except the creative Mind of God, and wills to create no limitation for himself. He is then "keeping his *high watch* toward *the one*."

Treatment follows this method: In the quiet of your soul, know with all the mind you can bring into action that God, desiring expression through *you*, gives you your true freedom, your thought medium being identical with His Mind. The same Law serves the Great Creator and the Specialized Creator, which is yourself. Know that to claim Peace and Happiness is to call out of the Law these experiences. Realize that there is absolutely no dividing line between you and God; that the freedom of God is your freedom. Then know that when you ask for guidance to speak only those words that will bring your happiness to you, this guidance will be an active directing force in your life and affairs. Consciously creating what you will to experience is divine freedom.

GOD'S WILL ABOUT HAPPINESS

Question—I prayed that a friend of mind might be united with me again, without result. If it is God's will for me to be unhappy, I will have to submit. I don't think it is any use to pray any longer.

ANSWER—It is never the will of God or universal harmony to have any person suffer. To do so would be to contain within itself—harmony—an element of inharmony, which of course is an impossibility. We are taught that God is Love and that in Him we live and move and have our being. Get this firmly fixed in your conscious mind: that God knows nothing about unhappiness. But since you are a free choosing agent and permit it to manifest, it will cause you suffering. Remember, you choose, and the law fulfills. Whatever it is that seems to separate you from your friend, if you will love that friend with no other desire than his happiness and perfect freedom, and if you set apart a time each day for the practice of unselfishly loving that person, the whole situation will clear. Know that if it is right for you to have this particular desire made manifest in your life, it will be brought into your experience at the right time and in the right way. Know definitely that there is no misunderstanding in Divine Mind.

SUBJECTIVE MIND

Question—What is subjective mind? How do we present a picture to it?

ANSWER—Our subjective mind is our mental emanation in Universal Subjectivity; it is our individual use of mental law. It is also the avenue through which Instinctive Man works, carrying on the functions of the body, for it is the silent builder of the body. The subjective mind of the individual is the working of Instinctive Man within him, plus all of his conscious and subconscious experiences. It is the seat of memory and of instinctive emotion. It contains a remembrance of everything that has ever happened to the outer man.

This memory is perfect and retains every experience of the individual life. It also contains many of the family and race characteristics which have been experienced by individualized man. It retains these memories, partly at least, as mental pictures or impressions.

We impress, or present, a picture to the subjective mind merely by thinking. Also, we present a picture through the function of seeing. Visualizing our desire into mind is nothing more than seeing in the mind the completed definite thing we wish to objectify.

POWER OF THE SUBCONSCIOUS

Question—What part does the subjective mind play in the normal operation of the human intellect?

ANSWER—The subjective mind is not an entity, but a storehouse. It is not a thing of itself but a *way* according to Law. It is a neutral field, responding to the intellect. It acts as a law of tendency, tending to reproduce in the objective world the images and states of consciousness which are imparted to it through our mental reactions to life.

SPECIALIZING THE LAW

Question—In what does the specialization of a natural law consist?

ANSWER—By the specialization of a law is meant the conscious use of that law for a definite purpose. We do not create the law. The law is used that it may create something for us. We generate electrical energy, we do not create it. We bring it to a center and distribute it. That which was simply a potential energy now has a definite purpose. It is not conscious of this purpose, but we are conscious of it. The energy of mind is similar to other laws. We are thinking centers in mind. The law of mind specializes itself through our belief. Faith generates the power, gathers it in. The treatment distributes it so that in one place it heals and in another place it is creative of conditions, etc.

WHY IS THE SPIRITUAL OBSCURE?

Question—Why is the spiritual obscure and the material seemingly so much more necessary in life?

ANSWER—The reason why the material has seemed more important to your life is because you could see only the material. You did not know that the very essence of the material thing you can see is Spirit. You have accepted mentally only that which you have known by your senses, not realizing that the thing itself, within the form you saw, was not and could not be discerned by the senses. Spirit surrounds us in people and in things—in the very atmosphere. But we miss all the joy and comfort of Spirit if we do not know it is there. When we look at the material world and realize its importance to us, *we are really looking at Spirit in form and action.*

INCREASING ONE'S RECEPTIVITY

Question—How may one's receptivity be increased?

ANSWER—One can increase his receptivity through definitely saying and feeling the truth of what he is stating that, "there is that in me which knows, understands, accepts, believes, recognizes and embodies. I know and I know that I know. I believe and am conscious that I believe. I am confident of the power of my own word, have implicit reliance upon the truth. I expect the truth to operate. This truth that I know is made manifest in my experience." Thus one gradually becomes more and more conscious of a Divine Presence, Power and Law responding to his word.

DENYING SENSE IMPRESSIONS

Question—I have been puzzled by the attempts of some philosophies to deny sense impressions. This does not seem reasonable to me. Does Religious Science deny or discredit the evidence of our senses?

ANSWER—If we denied the evidence of our senses completely, then by what criterion would we judge anything correctly? Religious Science does not deny the evidence of the senses, but of course does affirm that the senses are not always to be relied upon, which proposition you will readily prove from your own experience. It is not necessary to deny the physical world, nor any experience in it in order to demonstrate the truth.

PART II

The Nature of Mankind

MEANING OF POSITIVE THOUGHT

Question—What is meant by positive thought?

ANSWER—The word is dangerous. Many people mistake positive thoughts for will-power. The most positive statement one could make would be to say, "I am a human being." He would not wave his hands, pound the table and scream such a statement. He has no doubt about his statement and no denial can alter it one particle. So it is with our affirmations about the nature of our being. It is not by screeching and screaming that we are, but it is in the quiet contemplation of that *which we are* that our strength is.

THE FALLACY OF FATE

Question—Should we accept the belief in fate or destiny?

ANSWER—Certainly not. Our idea of the Karmic Law is one of cause and effect. We do believe in a specialized dispensation or a specialized creation. For example, we do not believe that the Universal Intelligence desired to tell an Edison all about electricity. This would be a special dispensation of Providence. On the other hand, an Edison wishing to know about electricity specializes in this subject. This is a specialized dispensation. To believe in a special dispensation would be to take away the incentive and the genius of individualism, which would rob man of incentive and selection.

THOUGHT AND IDEA

Question—What is the difference between a thought and an idea?

ANSWER—From the viewpoint of this question, a thought is a conscious act of the mind, while an idea is an actual subjective embodiment. How we get our images of thought, is the greatest single philosophic problem. Do we get them from outside or do they come up from inside? The external object is recognized because it awakens an intuitive perception which must have been inherent before it awakened. In reality there can be but one mind in the universe. In this mind is contained everything that was ever thought or perceived. From it will flow all ideas that are now inherent within it. Any demand made upon it creates a new idea. When we say that everything exists in mind, we do not mean in our conscious thought but in the Universal Mind. Our thought interprets this Mind. Our images of thought, even though they appear to be external, really come from within.

RIGHT AND WRONG THOUGHT ANALYZED

Question—How are we going to know what thought is right and what is wrong?

ANSWER—Our criterion is this—any thought resting upon the premise that there is One indivisible and perfect Presence which is never allied against Itself or against anyone or anything, that the only thing issuing from this is goodness, truth, and beauty and that this is all there is—that thought is always right. In our personal experience and for and about others, our thought will always be right if it is willing for anything that we think of, or about, others to be or to become true about ourselves.

POSITIVE AND NEGATIVE THOUGHT

Question—How is it possible to think both negatively and positively with the same mind, if mind is God?

ANSWER—Negative and positive thinking are merely two ways of using the same mind through the power of self-choice.

FINITE OR INFINITE

Question—Is man's mind finite or infinite, and is it possible for a finite mind to understand the Infinite?

ANSWER—Man, being the expression of the inifinite life, has within himself all the attributes of that infinite, and as he evolves, he uses consciously more and more of the infinite wisdom in the great encompassing and impregnating mind in which he "lives, and moves and has his being." In the sense that he is conscious only of certain fields in his experience, we say that his mind is finite—but the truth is that his mind is the very mind of the Divine Infinite, Itself. In the circumscribed fields through which man walks to round out his experience, he uses as much of this Infinite mind as he, as an instrument of All-Mind, is capable of sustaining at any time. But as he grows in understanding, he comes into wider and wider fields, and is conscious of more of the ultimate truth. But he can never comprehend the true Infinite until he reaches his ultimate Godhood and delivers his individuality to the Whole completely. Man always uses Infinite Mind, because there is no other mind to use. There is but *one Mind,* and one Law which all people use, consciously or unconsciously, constructively or destructively. . . . There is only One Ultimate Reality, but within this One there are many experiences. Man is within the One and draws from It any and all experiences in which he believes.

LIVING AFFIRMATIVELY

Question—Just what is meant by "living affirmatively"?

ANSWER—One who determines to live affirmatively has chosen to see only Good in everything, to have faith in that great *inner something* which animates him, which guides, directs, and loves him with a love beyond his understanding, and which fulfills his every desire and supplies his every need.

If conditions on the objective seem adverse and limiting, the person living affirmatively, deliberately and persistently ignores them as things having no power to affect him. He proceeds to change them by looking through them and postulating his thought in Original Cause. When his thought is so postulated, he lets it rest there, knowing that the law will do the rest. One who lives affirmatively is an unwavering believer in the goodness of life, the sureness of Divine Love and protection, the infinite care of the Creator for His creation. He is the master key to health, harmony and success.

GENERIC IDEA OF MAN

Question—What is the exact meaning of the Generic Idea of Man?

ANSWER—By the Generic Idea of Man, we mean the Original Creative Spirit, which, through Its nature, has pushed Itself forth through Creative Medium and Substance into the form which we know as Man. This Man, by his nature, is the image and likeness of the Universal Father, containing His every element and attribute. Man, then, is the actual Incarnation of Universal Spirit. There can be no man other than the incarnation of the original Creative Spirit—the incarnation of the Spirit in man, as man, is man.

TREATMENT

Question—Will the same treatment take care of or be effective for both health and prosperity, or must there be two different kinds of treatments given?

ANSWER—In the last analysis there is but one treatment given for anything that is desired. That treatment consists in convincing the mind that the thing desired is already accomplished. The only thing that seems to be difficult is for the person to *know that he knows* that what he asks is already his. Since man is of the Divine Substance, the quality of *knowing* is inherently active within him. But until man knows consciously that this inherent wisdom is at his command, he cannot use it consciously. Treatment is not for the purpose of making things happen; it is to provide, within ourselves, an avenue through which they may happen. Treatment opens up the avenues of thought, expands the consciousness, and lets Reality through; it clarifies the mentality, removes the obstructions of thought and lets in the Light. We already live in a Perfect Universe, but It needs to be mentally seen before It can become a part of our experience. Treatment removes doubt and fear, lets in the realization of the Presence of Spirit, and is necessary while we are confronted by obstruction or obstacles. Every problem is primarily mental, and the answer to all problems will be found in Spiritual Realization.

HOW TO DEVELOP REALIZATION

Question—How can one develop realization?

ANSWER—One develops realization through proof, gradually, a little here and there, in some slight way proving his Principle, gathering courage, proving a little more and on and on until at last he senses that he is dealing with Reality.

THE IMAGING FACULTY

Question—What is the technique for an expansion of the imaging faculty?

ANSWER—Your imaging faculty is mental, and all mental functions are of Mind, acting within Mind. If you can think of yourself as being able to imagine (or image) *whatsoever* you choose to create, and dwell in this contemplation, you will find your efforts to create mental pictures becoming much more fruitful, and less stressful. The limit of our ability to demonstrate depends on our ability to provide a mental equivalent for our desire. This mental equivalent is created entirely by the imaging faculty.

Your mental muscle grows by exercise, as does any other muscle. Picture your desires in a large, rich colorful way, and you will be exercising this mental muscle.

MEANING OF THE LAW OF AVERAGES

Question—What about the law of averages?

ANSWER—It is a law of experience which says that the average person will live about so long, eat about so much, sleep about so much, drink about so much and die at a certain time and will have in the life span a certain amount of happiness and a certain amount of grief. It is the consensus of human opinion about itself. We are subject to the law of averages as we are subject to the race thought until we free ourselves from it. By specializing the law of flotation, iron is made to float by the same law which makes it sink. So we specialize ourselves out of the law of averages by introducing a new mental equivalent which, while it does not deny the law of averages, lifts us somewhat above it.

MEMORY—CONSCIOUSNESS—PERSONALITY

Question—What is the value of remembering?

ANSWER—Memory is the only thing that binds personality

together in a sequential continuity. It is the only thing that makes possible a continuity. The value of any particular memory is probably simply the value by comparison. Memory itself becomes a subjective tendency no longer standing out in a clear and sharp outline relative to instances but becoming a tendency in life, deciding what is going to happen to our future and our acts. And so we find memory is a thing without which there can be no sequence of time, and without a sequence of time there can be no conscious experience. We are growing into a better consciousness but should this consciousness which we now have be entirely eliminated, *you would not be you* and the consciousness which you would have would be another thing entirely. It is necessary then that this thing is hooked up through all human experience.

UNIFYING THE SELF WITH THE WHOLE OF LIFE

Question—How can one who has always thought of God as being away from himself change his thought so that he can feel closer to life?

ANSWER—He must convince his reason that the Infinite must be an indivisible Unit. An indivisible unit must be present everywhere in its entirety, hence it must be in him. The Divine Being is within, outside, over-dwelling and indwelling him and responds directly to him by responding through him, so that he no longer speaks to a far-off God but to an interior Presence that fills all time and all space; but in him It is the Infinite Spirit of his own life and is his Spirit.

GIVING HELP TO OTHERS

Question—If a person has not removed from his own consciousness all sense of imperfection and has not demonstrated perfection in his own affairs, how can he help another person through a mental treatment?

ANSWER—We can help others insofar as we can sense their perfection in the Law and in the Spirit. It is entirely possible that one, even while he might be himself suffering, could help to relieve the suffering of another. If we all wait for the dawning of a complete realization of our inherent perfection, then we might have a long time to wait, and during the process of waiting nothing would have happened. The Law is, but we must direct It. And so far as the individual unity of life is concerned, it will remain undirected, other than through the law of averages, until a person consciously individualizes himself. I would not hesitate to help others simply because I had not, myself, attained a complete recognition of perfection.

SUBLIMATING THOUGHT DEFINED

Question—What is meant by sublimating thought?

ANSWER—This is a psychological term and means transmuting the emotional energy of desire into constructive channels, thereby eliminating the morbid secretion which is a result of a subjective accumulation of unexpressed desires. It is a freeing of repressed action, transmuting it and conveying its energy into other channels of self-expression. This energy is called libido or the emotional craving for self-expression back of all things . . . the repression of which leads to psychoneurosis, the sublimation of which heals this neurosis.

CONTROLLING ADVERSE THOUGHTS

Question—How can we learn to control adverse thoughts?

ANSWER—By consciously recognizing them as such, not fooling ourselves and saying they are not there when they are there, but by coming to understand that they have no power and then intelligently conveying consciousness to their opposite, nonresistantly but definitely. A direct statement in mind that a certain thought no longer has any power over us moves toward the neutralizing of that thought.

MEANING OF EMBODY

Question—What is meant by the word "embody" as used in the Science of Mind textbook? How may I embody the idea of active prosperity in my affairs?

ANSWER—The first thing to do is to invite and entertain the idea of your prosperity. This is building a mental equivalent. As your thought revolves about this idea, convince yourself that prosperity is your natural financial condition, your right to divine substance and supply. When you have convinced yourself of this truth you have "embodied the idea." You have impressed the thought-form into Universal Mind, which has accepted and believed your conscious mental projection as true. The voice of thought is your word—"In the [very] beginning was the Word,—and the Word was God."

For a realization of this truth, treat as follows: Know that there is no difference between your spoken word and the original Creative Word. Meditate on this until you feel assured of its truth. Then speak your word with authority for the objectification of prosperity, realizing that it has living power within itself, that it is its nature to produce.

NEUTRALIZING NEGATIVE THOUGHT

Question—Is it possible to erase an idea from the subjective mind to the extent that it is absolutely forgotten?

ANSWER—Psychologists tell us that is is impossible to absolutely erase an idea, that what we really do is to bring the idea to the surface and take its power away from it, so to speak; that while it is still a part of the memory, it is no longer destructive. When we speak of neutralizing, or erasing an idea we really mean erasing the possibility of this idea as any longer being a destructive power. It is probable that all thought impinged upon consciousness makes an indelible imprint. These images and impressions gradually become an accumulation on the subjective side of life. This backward stream of subjectivity becomes a generalized tendency, forcing itself forward again and molding the new objective streams of thought.

HOW TO SPEAK THE WORD

Question—Just how would one know what word to speak in giving a treatment, as there are so many different diseases and ailments?

ANSWER—In giving spiritual treatments it is not necessary to know the exact cause of any particular ailment. Indeed, it is impossible to always know the exact cause back of any particular disease. While we realize that everything moves from mind to matter, from cause to effect, or from the invisible to the visible, it is not necessary to know the exact cause of any particular manifestation in order to remove it. Spend little time thinking about the nature of the disease and more time in the realization of spiritual perfection; knowing that spiritual realization will find its own outlet for physical betterment.

DEFINITION OF ACTIVE FAITH

Question—"Faith without works is dead." What is meant by active faith?

ANSWER—A faith without works is merely a belief in a theory that you have not proved to be true. Active faith is the knowing, by experience, that your theory can be proved. When you can make no perceptible move toward proving that the universal good is yours, here and now, then is the moment for you to wait on God—to "keep thy heart [understanding] with all diligence, for out of it are the issues of life." (Prov. 4:23) Keeping one's heart high to the truth that God works in each and every one, is having active faith. It is only by standing unmoved in a condition that one may be master of it. As long as the problems of life make one desert the truth, just that long will a person find himself over-whelmed. You prove yourself stronger than the negative circumstance by staying positive to your Inner Self, and waiting patiently and with confidence on God. Such an attitude brings the desired results, and you have established your theory when the demonstration becomes an objective experience. In such case your faith has proved to be "the substance of things hoped for, the evidence of things not seen." Faith is an inner knowing. Faith *is real*. It cannot die. Man loses sight of it in stress, but it ever waits for him to rediscover it, and to put it to work for him.

CRITICISM

Question—When one criticizes another, does he put himself on the same vibration of inharmony and therefore easily attract criticism from others?

ANSWER—Yes, he does.

FAR-REACHING EFFECT OF TREATMENT

Question—Since there is only One Mind, would it not follow that in treating in that One Mind for any specific disease, such treatment would heal that disease in every person who has it?

ANSWER—Every treatment given is gradually neutralizing the race consciousness, finally helping to revolutionize the world order and promote a new one. Every specific treatment is a part of the accumulation of the sum total which will ultimately neutralize the belief and the experience of disease.

HOW TO PREVENT MAKING MISTAKES

Question—If sin is only a mistake and the inevitable conse-quence the only punishment, by what gauge can we recognize or predetermine a sin, and thus avoid making a mistake?

ANSWER—The predetermination mentally should not be in

the direction of "sin," so-called, but to its opposite, which is perfection. By keeping your eye single to the truth that *only that Truth which is your very life* can manifest through you and for you, and mentally accepting nothing to the contrary, you automatically forestall any tendency to make a mistake. It is this alone that is your work. When you have established within yourself that confidence that indwells you, you will have no fear. You will then act with the sure knowledge that there are no mistakes and that the One Infinite Mind is consciously directing your destiny. You will consciously *feel* the thing you should do. Treat to know that that point of Consciousness which is individualized in you and known in Mind by your name, is alive and aware *now,* and that It knows what to do, how to do it, and that It does it.

WHAT ANTAGONISM INDICATES

Question—What is wrong when one's disposition becomes antagonistic because of being unable to make a demonstration?

ANSWER—Antagonism indicates the presence of stress. The demonstration comes through peacefully when man relaxes in the situation and permits God to do the work. Man is prone to misuse his will. Will power is only the directing agency of Spirit, and not the creative agency. By faithfully knowing that God within him is doing the work, and by determining that no thought of his shall negate that spiritual fact, man frees himself from the burden and the stress that is father to his resentment against failure. This freeing from the burden, this conscious "letting" of the Spirit of his Good operate through him, is the demonstration in action. He cannot fail. Every thought-seed sown in mind has its own law of harvest. Know that if your demonstration is really necessary to your well-being, if it is truly a spiritual part of you, it projects itself into your experience for your use in time to serve you. In working it is well to say: "Father, I know this demonstration is given me, or its full equivalent, for the purpose of helping and serving my need." Believe what you say and do not forget that God's law imposes no burden on you.

MEANING OF THE SILENCE

Question—Just what is meant by the silence? Is this a necessary part of the treatment?

ANSWER—It means this: a contemplation in the quiet of the mind, when the objective tumult is temporarily stilled and we rise in our consciousness to the place of pure causation, which is Spirit.

MEDITATION ANALYZED

Question—How should one go into silent meditation?

ANSWER—Meditation *is* silent, since the very word symbolizes stillness as opposed to objective argument. There is a difference between going into the silence and meditating on some specific good or some specific quality or essence. Going into the silence does not mean making the mind a blank, and meditation is always some mental activity around a definite idea. For instance, take the thought of goodness. If one were going to meditate on this thought he would be conscious that he is meditating on the thought of *goodness* and he would be silently receptive to the idea which he is meditating upon. This might be termed an actively receptive mental attitude. On the other hand, if one were desiring to demonstrate a certain good in his life he would still be actively receptive on one side of his mind while being actively projective on the other side. That is, he would be knowing that this particular desire is actively expressed in his life. The mind can only take three positions: one of conscious receptivity, one of mental passivity, or an aggressive attitude. In any one of these positions we should always have some definite proposition in mind. In this way we protect our psychic life from undue intrusions.

INTUITIVE REALIZATION

Question—Is there such a thing as instantaneous intuitive realization?

ANSWER—Yes, there is. While most of our perceptions come gradually, there is such an experience as a quick flash of consciousness which realizes and accepts a universal truth without any process of reasoning. Many of our greatest truths have come to us in this manner.

EFFECT OF DOUBTS

Question—I am reading and studying and, I think, growing, but I get fogged and panicky occasionally when I look at conditions. I know I should not do this. Do we all doubt and become worried sometimes when the good that we. know is ours does not become manifested in our affairs? And do we then spoil all our work?

ANSWER—There is no one who does not become discouraged at times and at such moments the best thing to do is to divert the attention of the mind to some other interest. Believe these periods of discouragement are but temporary, that they have no real law to sustain them, and you will find that they gradually disappear as the mind becomes more and more certain of its alliance with pure Spirit. While it is true that all thoughts have power to manifest, it is also true that light has the power to dispel the darkness and one true thought dispels innumerable untrue ones. Do not be afraid of the negative outcome of your thought but dwell more on the positive side.

WHY TREATMENT IS NECESSARY

Question—If the Universal Intelligence is operating in and through us, why is it that It will not work for us without our treating for something to take place?

ANSWER—For the same reason that the desert does not produce; that electricity remains a potential, latent with the energy to run the machinery of the world, but first must be directed; because man is an individual, a consciousness with volition and choice, without which he could not be anything other than an automaton.

VESTED WITH DIVINE AUTHORITY

Question—I very much desire to "call out of the Universe that which is mine." Will you please tell me how to go about it?

ANSWER—First of all, realize that you are Incarnate Spirit, vested with Divine authority; that you may literally call your own and your own must respond, or obey the call. It cannot do anything else. Being a center in the Universe, you think or speak your word, and that thought and word is present simultaneously at every point in the Infinite Mind of the Universe. Your "call" becomes the living nucleus about which the answer gathers and forms. It is the nature of the law to evolve the right conditions out of the desire for its fulfillment. Realizing this, your responsibility ends with your call. God, Infinite Spirit, "speaks, and it is done." Man, Incarnate Spirit, therefore, speaks and it is done. In treating for your fulfillment, know that there is but the One Mind, the action of which transmutes your call into the right answer, your desire into the logical fulfillment. Your conscious recognition of the truth will serve to keep your purpose clear of confusion, and your mental force definitely directed. When you have convinced yourself that *you* speak and it is done, because the law *must* obey your word, you will never doubt.

CONSCIOUSNESS AND SOUL

Question—What is the difference between the soul and the consciousness?

ANSWER—Soul is the subjective part of consciousness, the psyche, the creative medium. Soul is consciousness, but consciousness is more than soul, for it takes in the self-conscious as well as the subjective.

THE DIVINE URGE

Question—How can I let the Spirit work through me? How can I discriminate between a Divine Urge and a human impulse?

ANSWER—The first thing for you to do is to recognize your unity with the great Universal Expression. If you can get a clear concept of your oneness with It you will be able to differentiate between the human impulse and the Divine Urge. For in the former, you will see that only the smaller self will benefit through the fulfillment of your desire, while in the latter, you will discover that what benefits you will be beneficial to all. Although the Universal Urge works through the individual, It never loses sight of Its own cosmic purpose. Therefore, you may ask yourself whether only selfish ends are served by the fulfillment of the desire within you. If you find this to be the case you may be sure that your human impulse is father to the desire. The Divine Urge is altruistic, serving the many through Its least expression. It deals with spiritual factors, such as love and service for their own sake; It is true to Itself on every plane of Its expression. To let this spirit work through you it is necessary that you find that secret place within your soul where you realize that your identity as an individual is simply the working of the great Self-knowing Mind. From this inner sanctuary analyze your impulse, whether it be the petty personal or the great Impersonal.

ACTION OF THOUGHT

Question—Where do you draw the line between holding thoughts and sending them out?

ANSWER—We neither hold thoughts nor send them out. We think them.

PASSIVE ACTIVITY

Question—What is meant by being passive yet also active?

ANSWER—To be passive and also active means to be non-resistant to those vibrations which are inimical to our peace, while at the same time we declare for the condition that we desire.

In practicing passivity to undesirable conditions, one should be very certain that he is not merely enduring them and hiding the fact from himself. While in the midst of things he seems unable to change to his liking, he must practice knowing with all the God-mind within him that the condition he desires is present in its fullness. It is present in his consciousness, complete and perfect. If he can realize this truth nothing can keep back the perfect manifestation. The invisible precedes the visible always. A person who is actively conscious that the invisible perfection is present, while being to all appearances in the midst of imperfection, is practicing activity while being passive to the imperfection. In his essay on Spiritual Laws, Emerson says: "I see action to be good, when the need is, and sitting still to be also good." In our mind we may sit still in undesirable conditions and at the same time be very active in creating desirable conditions.

CONSCIOUS AND SUBCONSCIOUS DEFINED

Question—Which has the most power, the conscious or the subconscious?

ANSWER—The conscious mind has the power of volition and of will. The subconscious cannot initiate a new chain of mental causation. But the subjective mind is infinite in its capacity to know and to do as compared to the objective mind.

MEANING OF HUMAN EXPERIENCE

Question—What is the meaning of human experience?

ANSWER—Human experience is a play of Life upon Itself, a result of the necessity of the Self-Expression of the Universal Mind and Spirit. Reality would not be real unless It were expressed. The entire physical universe, including man, is an expression of Self-Pronouncement of a Universal Reality, conscious of Itself through Its manifestation. Man is the highest form of this Self-Pronouncement known to the human mind, and since the higher form of intelligence invariably governs the lower, man is automatically given dominion over nature. Man's greatest exercise of this dominion is in the control of his own consciousness, for his consciousness in turn creates his destiny.

WHY WE BELIEVE IN IMMORTALITY

Question—Is it not true that remembering is the faculty in us which causes us to believe in immortality?

ANSWER—No. The thing that causes us to believe in immortality is life, which cannot conceive of death, or non-existence. It is fundamental, primordial, original, life itself, and that is why it is that there comes a time when people no longer think of immortality as such, as though it were a thing to be gained, for immortality is now. "If a man keep my saying, he shall never see death." They learn that they live. Immortality *is*, just as much now as it will be after we think we are dead and so it is that instinctive life in us, that knows nothing about dying, causes us all to believe in an endless existence. People believe in immortality unless they are educated otherwise. It is instinctive.

EXPRESSING THE REAL SELF

Question—What can I do that will enable me to express my real self in a constructive manner?

ANSWER—Your real self is the One Great Self. Your desire to express this Divine Purpose of your individual being is but the innate urge of the Great Self pushing forth into your consciousness. In this way It calls your attention, your mind, into cooperating with It. You should gather all your mental power into one vitalizing current and turn it on each of the activities you bring into your conscious mind for consideration. The moment it plays on the right or the Divine Purpose within you, you will sense a quickening which will serve to hold your interest on that point. Then daily treat yourself as follows:

"Divine Intelligence within me and within this point under my consideration, I recognize Your Presence, and I know You now reveal to me the avenue through which I find my perfect expression. Within this Word is each agency that is necessary to fulfillment and I know that, for the sake of the Self within me, I am now answered and satisfied. I expect and receive my answer and I am protected against making mistakes."

Meditate daily on the activity you have chosen, using the

treatment as given, and without doubt you will find new avenues opening to you. Fearlessly follow your hunches in connection with your meditation. Leave nothing undone.

NEUTRALIZING THOUGHT

Question—How can one neutralize thought?

ANSWER—By realizing that a thought is a real thing and that an opposite thought has power to dissipate its effects.

THE MENTAL EQUIVALENT

Question—What exactly do people mean when they say that your demonstration can only be equal to the mental equivalent embodied in your desire?

ANSWER—A demonstration, like anything else in the objective life, is born out of a mental concept. The mind is the fashioning factor, and according to its range, vision, and positiveness, is the circumstance or experience. For example: If a person can see only unloveliness in others, it is because unloveliness is a strong element in himself. The light he throws on others is generated in his own soul and he sees them as he chooses to see them. He holds constantly in his mind a mental equivalent of unloveliness and creates unlovely reactions toward himself. He is getting back what he is sending out. If a man believes himself to be a failure, and that it is useless for him to try to be anything else, he carries with him constantly the mental equivalent of failure. So he *succeeds* in being a *failure*, according to the law. That is his *demonstration*.

Having a strong picture or mental concept of that which we desire and holding to that mental equivalent regardless of circumstances or conditions, we must sooner or later manifest according to the concept. For in time the conception comes, through evolution and law, to the moment of birth, or projection into the objective world. Such is the way of Nature. Such is the law of all creation.

INHERENT AFFIRMATIVE THOUGHTS

Question—Do we have any inherent affirmative thoughts?

ANSWER—The great affirmations of life are both inherent and affirmative. That is, they are proclamations of the Universal Mind through us. All truth is inherent.

WHY DO WE GROW OLD?

Question—We are told that there is no such thing as age in the Divine idea of things. Then why do we, being Divine incarnations, experience age and growing old?

ANSWER—Divine Law says: "Ye shall have the land *ye see.*" So if man sees age as a human attribute, he shall experience it. Man cannot redeem himself and his experience from the race-consciousness of age and decay until he evolves to the plane above it. In this higher mental plane his thought will begin to sense the truth that Divinity is all there is in anything that is created, since Divinity is the sum total of *all* life.

Therefore, we see that as long as man believes that age is natural to human experience, he is functioning in the race-consciousness where this idea lives and acts its life out in human experience. He does not know himself. He has not accepted his kingdom. He is like the Prodigal Son, "afar off." Divinity in man knows Itself, and knows man *as Itself,* but It gives man choice and privilege as to beliefs and mental acceptances. Functioning through man as Divine Law, It fulfills man after his own mental images of himself. But the Divinity remains unsullied by man's error. Divinity evolves man's consciousness and in the evolution man discovers his error and discards it.

THE POWER TO DEMONSTRATE

Question—As we reach higher levels in consciousness do we gain more power to demonstrate?

ANSWER—Undoubtedly. The more inclusive the consciousness the greater its possibility. One can give only what he has; if he wishes to experience more, he will have to become more.

THE WILL AND THE IMAGINATION

Question—What are the relative parts played by the will and the imagination in treatment?

ANSWER—One is just as important as the other. Without direction by the will, imagination becomes mere day-dreaming. The imaging faculty of the mind is creative; it builds and molds, makes the mental form, conceives the desire consciously or unconsciously. When the imaging faculty is used in treatment of illness or inharmony, it recognizes only the true body of perfection which the Perfect Life made. Holding the patient in this recognition of perfection is the work of the will for his healing. He is consciously connected by the practitioner with his own good.

NECESSITY OF POSITIVE BELIEF

Question—Why did Jesus say, "Go and tell no man"?

ANSWER—He knew that the consciousness of the man whom he had just helped could very easily slip back into its negative state by listening to any denial of his healing. His thought, not being substantial enough, might become submerged by negative suggestion.

"RESIST NOT EVIL"

Question—What is the meaning of the saying, "Resist not evil"?

ANSWER—Nothing on earth can resist an absolutely non-resistant person. The Chinese say that water is the most powerful element, because it is perfectly non-resistant. It can wear away rock and sweep all before it.

When Jesus said: "Resist not evil," he knew the Father to be All and to be Good; he realized that all the power so-called evil had, was that which was given it by man. Not being a creation of God, it had no real life, no entity, but would affect a man's life so long as man believed in it as a power. Seeing through evil, or the illusion, to the truth, he counselled non-resistance.

Religious Science recognizes the power of Mind to build according to the belief held in It. Therefore, following the advice of Jesus, it refuses to believe that evil has any reality of its own, but that its only claim to existence is that given it by the belief of man.

Evil is *man-created,* while God, the Eternal Goodness, knows nothing about it. He is too pure to behold evil and cannot look upon it. Evil is the direct and suppositional opposite to good and has no reality behind it or actual law to come to its support. God tempts no man.

SUBJECTIVE MIND

Question—How do we know that the subconscious mind does not know what it is doing?

ANSWER—Everything that we know about subjective mind tends to prove that it is a doer and not a knower.

PROTECTION FROM MENTAL SUGGESTION

Question—What process of reasoning can make one immune from mental suggestion?

ANSWER—Know that there is but One Mind, that this Mind is constructive, and that nothing in the way of destructive influence can emanate from It. Say, for example, "I am surrounded by this Mind, protected by It. There is no hypnotism nor mental suggestion nor outside influence which can operate through me. Only that which emanates from the One Mind, only that which is in line with the One, can operate through me."

INDIVIDUAL USE OF UNIVERSAL POWER

Question—How is it that an individual, who is only a part of the Whole, can direct this Universal Power?

ANSWER—Just as an individual who is only part of the Whole can breathe the wholeness of the air and partake of the wholeness of the sunshine; just as a mathematician who is not the principle of mathematics but who is in unity with it, has access to the totality of numbers.

INDIVIDUALITY OF THE SOUL

Question—In the ultimate, can any outside force or any other personality or even oneself, harm one's soul?

ANSWER—In the long run nothing can harm the soul. In the long run it is bound to arrive. It is a part of God individualized and it must return to its Source in full possession of its individuality. We can hasten this completion by conscious choice and cooperation with the law.

HOW TO CONCENTRATE

Question—I have a lot of daydreams, but seem to lack will power, or mental ambition to carry them into action.

ANSWER—Will is a directive force, and when thus used it becomes the instrument through which Divine energy is directed. Teaching oneself how to meditate and how to concentrate takes as much practice as that required for any other accomplishment—*it is not done overnight.* Each day, without fail, give time to meditation—sit quietly, forget everything that suggests chaotic conditions or personal dilemma.

Each time a negative thought presents itself to you, discard it from your mind. Do not be discouraged if at first your mind seems to wander—persistently put every diverse thought out of your mind until you have formed the habit of controlling your own mental action. Know that perfect order and harmony in your affairs is your birthright and *claim it now*. Treat something like this: "Divine Mind within me knows all things. It knows the answer to my problem and this Mind makes me know consciously just what action to take. I listen for the inner guidance, and I do make the right decision, and that which is for my highest good is now manifesting in *all* of my affairs. I know that the Spirit of Infinite Goodness harmonizes into right action everything in my affairs, and that absolute Intelligence controls every act of my life."

OVERCOMING INFLUENCE OF OTHERS

Question—How can one build up a defense against the influence of others?

ANSWER—By knowing that he is not subject to the law of suggestion, thought transference or personal influence.

CHAOTIC THOUGHT

Question—I am practically well physically, but seem unable to get hold of things mentally. I am an educated professional woman. Please help me to find myself again.

ANSWER—If you mean that your mental world is chaotic or disorganized, the treatment for you to use is as follows:

Sitting quietly, contemplate the idea of your unity and harmony with Divine Mind; then realize that only harmonious and logical action and reaction can have place in this One Mind. You are one with this Mind, hence only your perfect good can reach you through Its channels. When you can sense the truth that this One Mind is your mind, declare your

Oneness with It. And on this basis, claim as your own all the mental power that this Mind has. Say:

"I know there is only One Mind, and It is my mind now. Hence my mind is in perfect balance. It is trustworthy. It knows what I want and gives me health, peace, power. There is nothing in me to deny nor delay the working out of my good, and I know it."

Praise God and know that it is finished, complete and perfect.

WHEN DOUBT PERSISTS

Question—When we know that we know and still a doubt comes up, is it because a subjective denial still remains?

ANSWER—The intellect often accepts only to find a subjective denial of its acceptance. It knows what it believes, it feels that it believes while at the same time it does not believe. This is a subjective denial of the conscious affirmation. It will gradually wear away and will no longer come to the surface—then knowledge will be more sure.

LOSING THE TRAIL

Question—I'm not sick or I'm not in trouble of any kind, but for some reason I don't seem to advance as I should. I have no trouble in holding a job, but I only advance so far and then stop. I have been studying Science of Mind for several months and only get so far, then stop—seems like I come to where the trail is dim, and I become lost and just wander around, accomplishing nothing. Will you please advise me how to get over or past this place where I always lose the trail?

ANSWER—It would seem that this losing the trail and groping about in confusion is a well-beaten habit-track on the subjective side of your life. It should be handled exactly as any other undesirable habit. If advancement is what you desire, you have but to know that even before the desire could present itself to your conscious mind, it had already taken on definite form. We are taught that supply precedes demand—"Before ye call, I will answer and while ye are yet speaking, I will hear." To wipe out the old habit, turn your mind to the new purpose—that of getting beyond the old mental stopping place. Realize that the infinity of the One Mind is resident within you—perfect, complete and powerful. Know that progress is the immutable law of your good and that there is nothing in the universe that can hinder or delay your advancement. Treat yourself as follows:

"I know that the One Perfect Mind, in which is everlasting and infinite advancement, is my mind, and It knows exactly how to carry me beyond the old point of confusion. In this Mind there is no confusion, no doubt, no hindrance, no obstruction, and all of these negative thoughts are now erased forever from my mind. By the power of this word which I speak for my advancement, I know that the immutable law of God waits upon my living word, to fulfill it." Daily practice will obliterate the old subconscious tangle.

HIT-AND-MISS THINKING

Question—After a lifetime of hit-and-miss thinking, how do I change to a life of constructive thinking?

ANSWER—We have a right to choose what we shall induce in Mind. The way that our thoughts are to become manifested, we cannot always see; but we should not be disturbed if we do not see the way, because effect is potential in cause. Cause and effect are really One, and if we have a given cause set in motion, the effect will have to equal the cause. Begin where you are—take stock. Hit-and-miss thinking lacks the effectiveness of a real plan. Vagrant thoughts finding lodgment in the mind will never result in anything useful because they are vagrant and not organized into a definite desire. If you would change your life to a constructive activity, deliberately choose some objective or goal you wish to attain and accept it mentally as being already attained. Instead of vagrant thoughts, definite thoughts along this particular line of fulfillment will come into your consciousness because you have set the law of projection or fulfillment into action. Ideas will flow into your conscious mental field because you have opened the way for them. When, from habit, the old haphazard mental pictures present themselves to your consciousness, definitely put them aside and turn your attention to your new picture.

ORIGIN OF THOUGHTS

Question—Where do our thoughts or concepts come from?

ANSWER—Our thought is motivated largely by a subjective accumulation of belief and desire on the part of the whole race, operating through us. It is also motivated by a cosmic purposiveness which is inherent in everything. Our ideas come both from a human and a Divine source.

FEAR OF ANOTHER'S THOUGHT

Question—Please tell me how to avoid being affected by the thoughts of others.

ANSWER—Work for mental stability, which is the ability to "stand" in your own mind without being "blown by every wind, and tossed." "Stand ye still," which means *stand ye steady*. In establishing this mental stability, you must be careful that the element of rigidity does not enter, because inflexibility of mind, wherein one becomes opinionated and arbitrary, is as great a fault as the other extreme or lack of the ability to "stand." The habit of being affected by the thoughts of others is negative and should be overcome. Treat as follows: "There is but one objective and one subjective mind. There is no mind stronger than mine; no mind can affect me against my judgment or my will. My judgment is at the helm of my thinking processes and protects me from the influence of other minds. Those things which I would not choose cannot enter my mental realm to affect my experience. This is the word I give to my subjective, in full faith that it strengthens me in my own positiveness and protects me from undesired suggestion. I know that I am protected and governed by Infinite Love and I am now free from all false suggestion.''

NECESSITY OF CONSTRUCTIVE THINKING

Question—Is constructive thinking necessary to spiritual development?

ANSWER—Spiritual development is the unfolding consciousness of our unity with good. Constructive thinking alone can sense this unity of good. Destructive thinking is based upon the supposition of duality. Constructive thinking is positively essential to spiritual development.

USE OF WILL POWER

Question—In the Science of Mind *Magazine, I find an article that makes me wonder if I have not been making the wrong use of will power. I cannot quite grasp it. What is the right way to use will power?*

ANSWER—The will is not creative but is a directive force. It is an instrument of the intellect, not of the imagination. When the imagination and the will are in conflict the imagination invariably wins. This is because emotion strikes deeper in the wellsprings of being than does the intellect. We do not will things to happen, and yet a man without will would be like a log adrift on a current. Use your will in making decisions and your feeling and imagination in backing them up.

MENTAL CAUSES OF DISEASE

Question—Can you give the mental equivalents or causes of various diseases such as cancer, sore throat and colds, bronchitis, asthma, indigestion, neuritis and rheumatism, nervousness, neurosis, etc.?

ANSWER—I do not believe that it is possible for anyone to state an absolute mental equivalent for physical disorders, since no two people react alike to the same emotion. It is admitted, however, by those who have made a study of the situation, that could we remove all sense of fear a majority of our physical ailments would be entirely eliminated. It is thought by many that very sensitive people are subject to throat affections; that congestions often follow confused states of mind; and it is generally conceded that mental conflict produces neurosis. But all of these wrong conditions will disappear in such proportion as we embody the spirit of harmony and wholeness.

EXPLANATION OF "BEING BORN AGAIN"

Question—What does the Bible mean by being born again?

ANSWER—Jesus said, "Ye must be born again." His disciples asked, how can this be? And Jesus answered, "Ye must be born of Spirit." We must have a spiritual rebirth. We must be born out of the belief in externalities into the belief of inner realities; out of the belief that we are separated from God, into the belief that we are part of a Unitary Wholeness.

HELPING OTHERS

Question—How can I help another, who seems to live almost wholly in race-consciousness, to lift up his thought to a higher level?

ANSWER—In helping others the question arises sooner or

later: "Just how far may one go?" It is not possible to tear a bud open if we want to have the perfect bloom. We have to let the sun and air and wind—in other words, nature—do the work. So it is in working for another whose consciousness is not evolved to the point where he can appreciate what is being done. Each one of us is an individualized center in God-consciousness, and each is expressing himself at the level of his consciousness of God. Thus each one is free to work out his own destiny and, as certain as night follows day, we all must find our way back to the "Father's House." But you can do some very powerful work within yourself which will embrace him and his unfoldment. You can follow the treatment given here and results are sure to follow. In your treatment, lift him to the plane of the absolute, knowing his perfection and that the love which fulfills all law fulfills him. Do not try to hasten his growth, but know within yourself that spiritual growth is ordained for him from the beginning of time and that he cannot resist its influence. Let all of your reactions toward him be affirmative; think of him constructively and see the constructive side of things habitually—that he is safe and secure in Divine Mind—and see him there perfect and complete.

FORCING A DEMONSTRATION

Question—In the attempt to demonstrate, when one discovers he is trying to force a desirable condition into expression, how should he go about just "letting" the demonstration come through? How may I "let my good come to me" without letting myself into a passive attitude?

ANSWER—You may save yourself from a passive attitude by positively knowing that your good is already accomplished, and by a wholehearted acceptance of it. Your responsibility ends with the recognition that it is *finished,* or involved, at the moment of your declaration into Mind. Evolution of the seed follows natural law. You plant a seed in the ground and *let* the law of growth evolve it into root, stalk, leaf and flower. It is just so with a mental seed. Do not keep worrying it to see if it has sprouted. "Let Patience have her perfect work."

GRATIFYING WRONG DESIRES

Question—If we have an urge to a certain expression, should we follow it, even if we know it to be wrong?

ANSWER—People who wish to do "wrong," knowing that they are setting themselves in opposition to the natural law of their peace, will of course expect to take whatever consequences present themselves. If it is necessary for them to suffer through gratifying wrong desires in order to disillusion themselves, it is an indication that their judgment is faulty, that they are in a maelstrom of mental recklessness.

Deliberately doing wrong is a flouting of the law of harmony, so the natural thing to expect in that case is inharmony of some kind.

The expressing of any wrongdoing is but the beginning of more trouble, and it heals nothing. Treat the tendency to such indulgence as follows: "God in me is good, and I in God am good. Therefore, in all my being there can be no desire to do wrong. Automatically I do good, think good thoughts and desire only good for everyone, for I realize I am one with everyone else. Love at the center of my being protects me from thinking other than thoughts of good. I rest in this realization, and am truly free and happy."

SUBJECTIVE EQUIVALENT

Question—Can you give me a clearer understanding of the term "mental equivalent"?

ANSWER—By mental equivalent is meant the subjective embodiment of an objective desire. To further explain: When the subjective state of our thought no longer denies our objective concepts, and insofar as these objective concepts are in accord with reality, then will our demonstrations be made.

MAKING POSITIVE DECISIONS

Question—What is the best way to overcome indecision?

ANSWER—Know, that "the mind in me, being the mind of God, knows what it wants to do, when it wants to do it, knows how to do it and does it. There is nothing in me that can defer or be afraid of meeting the issues of life exactly as they are." Indecision is often an unconscious camouflage which the mind projects to keep it from meeting a situation.

THE "STILL, SMALL VOICE" DEFINED

Question—Just what is this voice—"the still, small voice"? Is it audible or intuitive or a clear perception of thought, or does it take the form of conscious inspiration?

ANSWER—The "still, small voice" may reach one through the intuitive centers or it may seem to form actual words in the consciousness of the person entertaining it, and to give information that has been desired. It is the Inner Knowing faculty in man (in animal it is instinct). The "still, small voice" is a poetical phrasing for that Divine guidance which is within every created thing. The Universal Intelligence, which is at the center of every living creature, may be consciously called into immediate use. If one asks for this guidance he will be conscious in some way of the response. He will probably experience an "impression," a definite decision in a matter may make itself felt within him, or in some cases he may hear with his inner ear the actual words spoken for his guidance. Reality speaks within the consciousness of man when man allows It to do so, or whenever man calls upon It and consciously waits for Its response.

Man, being a center of God-consciousness, is never away from God. The more he turns within himself to find the truth about himself, the more will he develop his powers of inner knowing. Therefore, the more he relies on inner guidance for his daily life-experiences the keener will his perceptions be of the "still, small voice" through which his guidance comes.

PART III

Spiritual Healing

CONTROLLING NERVOUSNESS

Question—I am obsessed with a terrible fear of losing my mind. Every little thing disturbs me and I don't seem to have the manhood to conquer this nervous trouble.

ANSWER—We are told that we become like that unto which we look upon. So it is quite necessary for you to handle this fear that disturbs you. As you realize it is a nervous reaction, your work can be definitely handled, and daily practice will soon free you from this habit. Back in the subjective are the images of thought acting themselves out in our objective experiences, and it is there that this false image of obsession has taken hold; it, therefore, must be neutralized and destroyed by definite and specific work. Take up the work daily and say in your treatment: "There is only the One Mind—the Mind of God—and It knows I am *free* and *fearless*—free from this undesirable and usurping fear. I know this fear has no foundation, that it has no power or life in itself, and that it cannot stand before my neutralizing word. I know that my word spoken for my freedom from this obsessing fear is perfect and deals with a perfect law and frees me from all fear and sense of burden. I know that my word represents a perfect idea of truth. It has perfect life and establishes the law of peace and harmony, and restores me to complete normalcy. I know there is nothing in me that repudiates peace, for I am a center of divine Consciousness and *I am at peace.''*

HEARING

Question—Can you help me to attain greater harmony with the mental laws so as to improve my hearing, which is impaired?

ANSWER—Hearing is a divine idea in Mind and all divine ideas are perfect. Ideas have a service to render to the Spirit of man, and as long as man expects and accepts wholeheartedly that service, and cooperates consciously and subjectively with it, there is nothing to oppose the functioning of the physical instruments through which ideas operate. Treat to know that your hearing is perfect, that it is God hearing through you. There is no belief in inaction that in any way can hinder your hearing, for every idea of your body is now complete and perfect and functions according to the Divine Law. Be open and receptive to the Truth.

NO SEPARATION IN MIND

Question—I live in Santa Barbara, California. Can I help my brother in Nebraska recover from an operation which has been performed in a hospital there?

ANSWER—There is no separation in Divine Mind. Divine Mind is Omnipresent, Omnipotent, Omniscient, perfect and complete and It knows no particular geographical point as being near or distant. Realize the truth of this completeness and perfection at the point of call—the point of call then becomes the place where spiritual and mental work is done, since the individual "I" is included in the universal "I amness." Thus you can see that your brother can be reached as effectively in a Nebraska hospital as can a person sitting within reach and hearing. Mind is immutable and eternal and what It knows at one point It knows at all points at the same instant and with the same force.

TRIES TO LET GO

Question—How may I learn to let go? I have been reading and studying for three years. I feel sure I am receptive and understand the fundamental truths, but somehow do not manifest as I should. I have been sick for years. I have done lots for myself but am not where I should be, and there must be a reason. Maybe I am too anxious.

ANSWER—Undoubtedly you have answered your own question. Perhaps it would be well for you to take your thought entirely off yourself and try to sense the harmony of being. It is often a good thing to remind ourselves that there is little to learn but much to realize. The truth itself is the essence of simplicity, since its whole teaching is that the life which we live is continuously a perfect state of being. This life flows into our being and becomes the substance of our body and affairs only in such degree as we embody it. And in such degree as we do embody it, its flow through us becomes automatic. When the mind shall learn to reflect the essence of pure being, the body and affairs will react accordingly.

HELPING THE TUBERCULAR SON

Question—How am I to establish in my own consciousness a realization of health for my son who has tuberculosis?

ANSWER—In mental treatment one of the first things which a practitioner must do is to separate the false belief and condition from the one affected by it. You must try to think of your son as being the substance of pure Spirit, perfect in every part. If you are unable to do this you should secure the services of one whose practice and experience has enabled him to prove that this mental position demonstrates itself through a renewal of the physical body.

TO CORRECT STAMMERING

Question—How can one correct stammering? I would be unspeakably happy to be free from this condition.

ANSWER—To relieve the condition, a persistent, consistent practice of speaking deliberately will of necessity have to accompany the mental treatment. In your meditation, see yourself speaking freely and fluently. Say: "There is no hurry—no worry—no impatience—no congestion in pure Spirit. The Law of the Lord is perfect and is manifesting in and through me now as my perfection. Only that which is true of God is true of me, for I and my Father are one. I am deliberate action on every plane. I speak clearly and coherently, and my word is the natural expression of the One Spirit within me. There is no hindrance or obstruction. This so-called stammering has no power; it has nothing to sustain it; and my word here and now dissolves and destroys it." When the Spirit of Truth bears witness of *Itself*, the healing is instantaneous.

A UNIQUE EXPERIENCE

Question—My physical condition is very unyielding. The healing power of mental treatment seems to cause pain when directed to the affected parts. This seems to be a rather unique experience and I hesitate to mention it, but it is very real to me, however illusory it may appear to others.

ANSWER—Perhaps in your treatment you are recognizing the disease or the pain as being an entity and, in so doing, you focus your attention on the disease rather than on a state of perfection. I should not try to focus my attention on any infected parts but rather seek to realize a harmonious wholeness within and realize that this automatically flows into every part.

TROUBLED BY ASTHMA

Question—I have just listened to your wonderful radio message on "Faith" and was so impressed that I am writing to ask you if you will please tell me how to proceed to cure a very distressing case of asthma?

ANSWER—If you can learn to release the tension of your mind, I believe you will be freed from your condition. It is written that the breath of God animates creation with the living presence of a pure divinity. What breath, then, are we breathing, other than this true breath—unrestricted, flowing through channels of pure receptivity from the Infinite Intelligence and the perfect life of God? Let your thought dwell not on breath but on that which breathes; sense its freedom and you will be free.

CANCER

Question—How should I treat cancer?

ANSWER—In treating any form of false growth one should work to know that the spirit indwelling this patient finds a perfect, complete manifestation through him, that nothing has ever attached itself to his spirit, that every false shadow of belief cast into man's consciousness by any and every form of erroneous conclusion is now obliterated, is now completely erased, and forever wiped out. False growth is neither person, place nor thing; it cannot take root in the truth; it has no vitality, no substance, and no power and cannot be fed or nurtured by the truth. Pure and perfect light of Spirit dissipates and dispels any and every form which is unlike peace and harmony, "and the place thereof shall know it no more forever." This word is complete, perfect, breaks down every appearance of false growth, restores perfect assimilation, circulation and elimination.

INDIVIDUAL FREEDOM

Question—How would you meet a condition of too great a response to friendliness, such as well-meaning people who like to be with you so well that they absorb too much of your time?

ANSWER—I would work to know that my consciousness protects me and leaves me in perfect freedom to come and go as I wish, that no one in any way, shape or manner can absorb my time, thought or consciousness beyond that which I consciously wish to give. There should be no sense of criticism in this thought, just an absolute sense of one's own individuality, for the very thing that is being attracted is good of itself: the idea of friendship and love.

OVERCOMING IRRITATION

Question—As a business woman, I have always filled my position easily and thoroughly, but business life irritates me, makes me nervous and on edge. I have a constant inner desire for a quiet home and homely tasks. Circumstances seem to push my desire further and further away from me. After coming from another state, my fiancé has had constant difficulty in securing a satisfactory position and a reverse of conditions has made it necessary for me to support my mother. How can I use Religious Science to attain my desire?

ANSWER—The first thing you should do is to come into unity and harmony with your work. In all probability you are resisting things, while the injunction is to resist not evil and it will flee from you. Know that the spirit within you is directing and guiding you and that it makes straight the way before you, providing for every need and bringing into your experience everything which makes for your happiness. *Trust the Law to find Its own outlet.*

FEAR OF CONTAGION

Question—A little boy who had been a playmate of my two children died after a sudden and very short illness which was said to be highly infectious. I have tried to keep myself calm and unafraid, but have been alarmed for my children: How shall I treat?

ANSWER—Recognize that no belief of the human mind, acting through contagion or false suggestion, can in any way have power over you or your children. In the 91st Psalm it is written: "A thousand shall fall at thy side and ten thousand at thy right hand but it shall not come nigh thee." This is the platform on which you must stand firmly. Know from the very center of your being that "He hath given His Angels charge" over your children and that no harmful thing or condition can come nigh them. The Angels are your own protective thoughts in the realm of absolute Truth and they wrap them in invulnerable security. Speak your word for Divine protection for your children *fearlessly.*

Say daily: "No harmful thing can touch him (your child—*naming* him), for Divine Love protects him." Born of the Spirit, your child is changeless, perfect, and completely safe and secure in Divine Mind. Form your treatment in your own words and treat each child, believing your idea is the truth about them.

MENTAL TREATMENT FOR CHILDREN

Question—Is it easier to treat a child mentally than it is to give treatment to an adult?

ANSWER—It is generally easier to treat a child than an adult. The child has had less experience and is less marked, subjectively. Hence, there is usually a greater receptivity on the part of the child than there is in an adult.

OVERCOMING FAULTS

Question—Critical, intolerant, too impulsive and emotional, too severe and almost without love. I seldom line them up like this, as it is a formidable array which depresses me, and if that is self-pity, I am guilty of that, too. But how to overcome them?

ANSWER—Since you have climbed Life's Endless Stairway to the point of honest revelation and admission of your "faults," the next step is a decision to climb out of them, leave them, forget them. "Life is changeless in its endless change." There is nothing "set" in it. This is the point for you to work on. The hard shell which apparently encompasses you will break and fall away from you when you break through it. Persistent hammering on the same spot in any wall will break the wall. Every time the old intolerant attitude suggests itself to you, turn it squarely around and demand the right mental reaction toward the thing you would criticize. This practice, persisted in, will develop a "good-natured flexibility" in all your reactions which will prove to you that far from being "without love," Love is the very essence and core of you.

VISUALIZATION IN TREATMENT EXPLAINED

Question—To what extent does visualization enter a metaphysical treatment?

ANSWER—When giving a treatment, use any method and every method which will convince the mind, because that is what mental treatment is. There are certain instances where visualization is a great aid to this. By visualization is meant mentally seeing the accomplished fact. This is a legitimate part of a treatment—not a necessary one, but if it helps the mind to receive and to believe, it is good.

OVERCOMING APPARENT EVIL

Question—Should we know all men to be good, regardless of apparent evil?

ANSWER—We should know the truth about all men, and that is that they are made in the image and likeness of Divinity, with all the privileges and prerogatives to be found in Divine Law. We should recognize the Divine in them, no matter what the apparent seems to declare. The man who does not *know himself* to be indwelt by the Divine Cosmic Harmony will of necessity not function higher than his recognition of himself. If he is seeing two powers, good and evil, he has not discovered that the evil is simply the good misdirected. Since we live in all planes of Being, *manifesting* only that which we can embody mentally, it follows that the person who realizes that all men are good, regardless of appearances, is embodying for those whom he regards, the truth for them. Such recognition must impinge on the consciousness of the so-called evil appearance, and make itself felt.

CONTROL OF NERVES

Question—How should one think or feel when one is trying to rest and noise disturbs, such as small children crying and even playing boisterously? I feel I am getting better every day, but could make much more rapid progress if things would not disturb me so.

ANSWER—I should treat myself to know that there is no inner irritation or agitation, no confusion, and that I am always poised in pure Spirit. *Agree with your environment* and know that there is nothing which can disturb you.

JEALOUSY

Question—How may I be healed of jealousy, anger and resentment and of being critical and fault-finding; I just feel as if life is not worth living anymore.

ANSWER—Jealousy and resentment and a critical, fault-finding mind are the result of an inferiority complex accompanied by a super-sensitive nature. Do not try to hold anything to you or push anything away from you, but rather seek to know in your own mind that you are in harmonious unity with all things and all people. Try to sense the inner peace and completion arising from the wellspring of your own being. Nothing can be taken from or added to that which is already complete, and when we know that we are already complete, in such degree as we know this, we find that we are attracting a greater good into our personal experience. Try this and see what will happen.

UNBELIEF

Question—It is said that Jesus could do no great works among his own people because of their unbelief. Is it possible then to successfully treat those who are opposed to mental healing?

ANSWER—Jesus said: "As thou hast believed so be it done unto thee." If a practitioner were called to treat a case where the patient was not willing to cooperate, he would not take the case. For the practitioner understands that he has no right to coerce the patient, even for his own good. Surely no practitioner would so far deny individual freedom of belief or action as to force his own consciousness on one who opposed him. The thought for you to entertain for the opposing person is that he is a perfect idea of God. Simply keep him in the right light in your own understanding and know that he is safe and secure in God.

HOW TO BE SOCIABLE

Question—Besides an inferiority complex regarding not being able to meet and be sociable with people, I have had pains in the top of my head, with dizziness, and am depressed most of the time. Will you please help me to overcome this mental condition? Being radiantly happy would help overcome depression and the complex too, wouldn't it?

ANSWER—Yes, being radiantly happy would indeed heal your negative reactions to life, and since you have sensed that this is the golden key to your problem, the next step is for you to use it to unlock those centers of graciousness and true appreciation of your fellow man which lie within the soul. That inner, true self, which is really You, knows itself to be unified with the great invisible spirit of Life. It knows this Life to be pure radiant joy, love and happiness. It knows itself to indwell every human being as a vital spark, an individual point in Cosmic Consciousness, and it sees itself in every other individual. Take this Truth into your meditation each day, realizing that you can become whatsoever you can believe yourself to be. If you can accept the belief that you are a perfect, joyous idea in Divine Mind and that immutable law waits upon your wishes, you can change every mental picture of limitation into one of fulfillment. "Act as though I am and I will be." In treating the case, say:

"I know there is One Perfect Mind, which recognizes me as a part of Itself. I know the Mind which I use is the One Mind which everyone else uses. By this word which I know to be Pure Spirit, I erase all thoughts of inferiority and I rely on that inner Intelligence to uphold me on every plane of expression. All confusion and bewilderment and mental clouds are dissolved by my word, and all pain, dizziness and depression are erased; therefore, I am free to express life in perfect health and happiness."

PROSPERITY CONSCIOUSNESS

Question—How does one establish a prosperity consciousness?

ANSWER—A sense of prosperity with its accompanying beneficial result is established through the continual recognition that right and harmonious action is, and is ever flowing to us, through us, around us and everywhere. Do not try to make things happen but try to sense that the principle of life is producing right action in everything you do, say or think. When a cloud of confusion or doubt appears on the mental horizon, look at it until you know it has no power. Penetrate the mist of uncertainty with the firm conviction of reality until the mentality sees, even in the midst of confusion, an eternal peace and abundance. What a man has, as well as what he is, is a result of the subjective state of his thought. When the time comes that doubt no longer rises from your consciousness you will be free.

ELIMINATING FEAR

Question—How can we rid ourselves of fear? Would working for perfect love be enough?

ANSWER—There is no man living who has completely eliminated all fear or all hurt. It is our belief that when the time comes there is nothing in us that *would* or *could* do harm, we shall never again *be* hurt. But that is apparently quite a way ahead in our evolution. When the time comes in the life of any individual that he knows everything is all right, that there is nothing fundamentally wrong with the universe, he will cease being afraid. It will come to all of us somewhere, sometime. Until it does come, we must treat the present fear and always be tending toward the perfect goal.

NEURASTHENIA

Question—How should one use the Science of Mind in the case of a patient in a sanitarium who is afflicted with neurasthenia and who is fault-finding and quarrelsome and continually complaining, and who cannot be induced to make any effort to control her troublesome disposition?

ANSWER—Neurasthenia is the derangement of the nervous system with a depletion of the vital force. The dictionary gives the psychological cause as an inadequate expression of the libido. This means that those suffering from this disorder have not fully expressed their desires along constructive channels.

Remember that nervous disorders are very real to those suffering from them. They become fretful, have headaches and are generally out of harmony with life and with people. This is their disease. It is useless to call the whole trouble nothing but imagination. It is more than imagination, for it is a very real condition to the one suffering from it.

The great need of such people is for them to come into a realization of themselves, to become poised in their thought, to be made happy, to feel that they are one with a life that is good.

If you find that in this particular case you cannot talk about these things to your patient, the best method to use is to think of her as being poised and happy. Do this silently and overlook the apparent trouble as far as possible. Treat her, within your own mind, until you sense her poise and happiness.

Try not to think of her as being impatient but reverse your thinking and see her as calm, patient and lovable. *You will win along these lines.*

DUAL PERSONALITY

Question—My son seems to be obsessed by a dual personality. Do you believe in evil spirits and how do you interpret the many New Testament accounts of demoniac possession?

ANSWER—*There are no evil spirits.* There is one Spirit, and that is the All Harmonious Universal Essence. The demons spoken of in the Bible are just as much alive today as they ever were, only today we call them by another name. We speak of them as "*beliefs* in sin, sickness, poverty, etc." When Jesus cast out the devils from Mary Magdalene and healed the lunatic and performed all the other acts of healing to his recorded credit, he was merely handling the misbeliefs of the time scientifically. He did not try to convince the father of the lunatic that there were no such things as demons, but he "rebuked the devil; and he departed out of him, and the child was cured from that very hour" (Matthew 17). In other words, he handled the case as it was presented to him, thus maintaining a perfect mental harmony, recognizing *only* the One Mind, the One Power, the One Life in the boy.

The answer to the second part of your question, then, lies in this: Demoniac possession, as depicted in the New Testament, is a picturing forth of the destructive effects of wrong thinking and believing. It stands diametrically opposed to the fact that "The image of the Father cannot be defaced nor can all the wit or the sham of man really obliterate this image." Jesus, in his healing ministry, realized and proved the truth of man's relationship to the Divine Perfection.

WHEN DOUBT PERSISTS

Question—What should be the treatment when doubt persists in lurking in the mind?

ANSWER—When doubt persists the treatment should definitely repudiate this doubt. Doubt is a subjective state and is the result of false experiences and false conclusions regarding life and our relationship to the Spirit of Wholeness.

Thoughts are things, and mental attitudes assume the characteristics of entities until they are seen in their true light. When we recognize any special doubt and consciously show ourselves why this particular doubt has no power, we dissolve it.

It may take both time and patience to dissolve certain doubts and fears but the reward is sure if the work is done scientifically. Allow the doubt to come into your conscious mind and then analyze it out of your mind. Do this until you see that there is no power in the doubt. It is neither person, place nor thing, has no power and cannot operate through you.

Assume the opposite attitude and claim all confidence in yourself and in what you are trying to do. Rise above the doubt into a clear atmosphere of receptivity and agreement with the good you seek to manifest or to have manifested to you.

A good method is to drop all argument from the mind and allow the thought to enter a field of peace and poise. Having gained this point calmly turn to the disturbed idea and state that it cannot enter your mentality. Do not fight or oppose it but stand above it and declare that it has no power to operate through you.

TREATMENT FOR ENERGY

Question—How may one treat to correct a condition in which there seems to be little physical energy, or "pep"? Can lassitude be dispelled by mental treatment?

ANSWER—Lassitude is largely the result of the lack of enthusiastic interest in life. Become enthusiastic over something and you will find the lassitude will disappear. It is an abnormal condition. When we find some object or activity to which we can give our unreserved attention and enthusiasm, we thereby open the channels of life, causing a complete circuit of Spirit through us which automatically dispels inaction. You should treat yourself to know that you are drawn unto those situations to which you may give your entire enthusiasm.

COLDS

Question—Will Religious Science heal a common cold? If so, will you please tell me how to treat for this condition as I am very susceptible to every change in the weather?

ANSWER—Since you admit that you are susceptible to changes in the weather with the result that you have colds, you must be brought to realize that you have accepted this mental impression so whole-heartedly that every wind that blows plays upon you as upon a delicate harp, sure of accord with it. The trouble really lies not with the weather, but with your mind. Fear is at the bottom of it; perhaps old training has impressed you with the idea that a "draft will give you pneumonia." This belief causes you to be afraid and confused. But mental conflicts also cause confusion, and confusion causes colds. So search your subjective for the habitual source of your colds. You will, therefore, see that Religious Science can help you to heal yourself forever.

ACIDOSIS

Question—Kindly tell me what, in your opinion, causes acidosis, as it seems to be a popular disease.

ANSWER—It is not always necessary to know the exact cause of any particular disease. But to know that there is no reality to evil and no power in that which is false, is scientific. The Spirit is pure, undefiled, and It is the essence of kindness. There is no bitterness or vindictiveness in Spirit. It contains no condemnation and judges no one. You are Spirit. Perhaps there has been an unconscious negation working in your mind for some time. It would be well worthwhile to clarify your thought. Forgive all that appears to have been wrong. Hold no evil thought against anyone and see what the result will be.

DISSOLVING A FALSE BELIEF

Question—Please explain your method of dissolving a false belief.

ANSWER—A false belief is dissolved from the subjective by a repetition of the truth in its place. It is a right-about-face, a mental action in the opposite direction from the habitual one. A drop of clear water, repeatedly let fall into a bottle full of dirty water, will eventually show the bottle to be full of clear water. Repetition is the key.

A false belief, when recognized to be false, is displaced by a repetition of what you know to be true. Your first repetitions may seem to be mere intellectual statements in which your emotions play no part, but if the statement is repeated often enough, with the sincere desire to believe it, the moment comes when the last resistance "lets go," as the last drop of muddy water was washed from the bottle. It takes time, patience, and a determination to win, but the result is highly worthy of the effort.

IRRITATION OF THE SKIN

Question—I have a very irritating condition of my skin, which has continued for several years. When I was a young girl I had a similar condition for five years. An analyst has traced the case and finds the periods of skin eruption to parallel two experiences in my life when I was much disturbed by people with whom I was forced to live. Could that have been the cause and can it be healed by Religious Science?

ANSWER—We are taught that whatever is held in mind must come forth in form. If you have been irritated mentally and have not been able to adjust yourself to the undesirable cause of the irritation, it is but natural that it should manifest objectively sooner or later. On the other hand, you may be unaware of the cause, it being so deeply covered in your subjective that it has not come to your consciousness. Criticism and inability to live with people, to adjust oneself to the many, brings about many disorders. A deep-seated resentment against persons or conditions will surely manifest itself in the form of some disagreeable physical reaction. The first step toward healing is one of honest self-analysis: What has been your habitual feeling toward the persons around you? Have you really tried to *let them live as they see fit,* while claiming the same freedom for yourself? Watch with unrelenting zeal that no unlovely thought enters your mental world to register its residence. When you take your firm stand, and declare that "None of these things move *me!*" the undesirable conditions will drop away from you. Treat thus:

"The center of my being is Understanding and Intelligence, and It knows how to sweeten my experiences. I charge It with this ameliorating power and give thanks that my word brings back to me the sweetness I speak into it. I am whole, sound and perfect, in thought, act and body. I am cleansed from every thought that is contrary to that of love and tolerance."

FAILS TO HOLD FRIENDS

Question—Just recently I have become rather despondent, as the more I try to help myself, the worse I get. If I could ever overcome the worry about losing my dearest friends, I would be very happy.

ANSWER—Emerson says, "If you wish to have a friend, be

a friend." It is important that we should turn loose of our friends if we would keep them. Are we permitting something other than perfect freedom in thought, speech and action to formulate our reaction toward our friends? True friendship is founded on the principle of Unity. Feel the Spirit of Friendliness within you; it is an irresistible magnet and will draw friends to you. To have an enduring friendship, lasting and true, cultivate an attitude of friendship toward everybody and everything. Love more. Love is reciprocal and it gives back to us as we give to it. Daily build such an atmosphere of goodwill and friendliness around you that friends will seek you, and persistently image these ideal friendships.

The Law always works.

DISTRESSED BY DREAMS

Question—Can it be worthwhile for a person of age seventy to attempt to subdue that part of the subjective mind which causes a strange perversion to be manifested in dreams? My dreams are wholly unlike the life I live—a sort of low-brow personality always in some distressing mix-up, toiling to no purpose, alone and in want, childish fear of burglars, etc. I have studied to overcome this condition but nothing has improved that undercurrent of misery, or obsession, you might call it.

ANSWER—If you treat yourself each day to know that during the night your mind is undisturbed by any dreams and is at peace, you will, by making these definite statements, overcome the habit of problematic dreaming.

VICTIM OF CHRONIC WORRY

Question—Troubles and ill health seem to have made me a chronic worrier and I am extremely sensitive; my surroundings are not to my liking and the unhappiness seems to aggravate my physical condition. I can analyze myself, but

*never seem able to help myself. It is imperative that I regain
my health as I have an invalid mother to take care of.*

ANSWER—A chronic habit becomes such through a repeated
subconscious habit. A false sense of personal responsibility is
the parent-seed of the worry habit, and sensitiveness or
"nerves" is the logical result. Analysis reveals the error, but
a determined, persistent, definite practice in neutralizing this
condition by an opposite thought of truth is necessary for a
healing. Worry has brought neither health nor happiness.
Use the imagining and creative faculty of mind to free yourself of the habit. Each day see yourself well, active and radiantly happy, striving with all your understanding to "change
your mental concept." Practicing this as often as you can,
daily, will work wonders. Get a new frame in mind and put
a new picture in it.

ACQUIRING BETTER MEMORY

*Question—Will you please tell me if the Science of Mind will
help me to overcome self-consciousness and enable me to
remember better?*

ANSWER—The Science of Mind explains the nature of the
working of mind through its natural function of thought,
and it gives definite instruction on scientific methods of
treatment. The earnest study and a persistent practice of the
truths taught at the Institute of Religious Science will eventually carry your consciousness of self to its source, the Great
Self, in which are all the attributes of power. You will learn
how to let go of the small, limiting thought and to "think
largely." You will also learn how to treat yourself for improved memory.

Memory is the ability to remember things that have happened; therefore if something happened two years ago, of
which we are not at present thinking, we can remember it,
because it is in our subjective thought. When we say that we

are getting absentminded, it means that we cannot recall thoughts. A person may be healed of this belief by knowing that the One Mind never forgets Itself. This Mind is our Mind now.

TO EXPRESS LOVE

Question—How may one learn to express love toward others? It seems I cannot express love at all toward those I should, and still I know I love them. I seem cold and hard toward others, just not knowing how to get close to them, and always thinking maybe they don't want me or don't understand me.

ANSWER—Your problem is sensitiveness and a reluctance to express yourself. Probably you are both sensitive and conservative. Try to feel in your own thought that the love which goes out from you to others is reciprocated by them and comes back to you again. If you break down the intellectual formality in your own thought and sense the unity underlying all life until it becomes a part of your mental make-up, you will find the corresponding reaction will be a closer relationship with people and events.

INSTRUMENTS OF VISION

Question—I do not go to shows or read for any length of time, as I feel that to do so would be a strain on my eyes. Do you think that I am expressing fear, or am I doing what is best?

ANSWER—As long as you feel that going to shows and reading will strain your eyes, you should refrain from these indulgences. But in the refraining, you should take the time to sit in meditation. At this time you should definitely feel that your eyes are spiritual ideas, perfect in Divine Mind, which created them; and that this original idea of the organs of sight is also perfect, strong, vital and unimpaired in your own mind. You should practice *believing* that your eyes are the perfect instruments of vision, and that they are not subject to strain, fatigue or any other negative manifestation. This, however, does not preclude normal and sensible care and protection of them. If you feel that fear is a factor in the case, treat yourself for the elimination of fear in the subjective. Realize daily that there is no obstruction to vision, there is no weak vision, for there is only the One Perfect Vision, which is *now* seeing through you. Be definite and specific in your work.

HELP FOR A TIRED MOTHER

Question—How about a mother with three children? I do get exhausted. How can friction be eliminated in family life?

ANSWER—The crux of your whole problem is revealed in your closing sentence. The work to clear up this entire situation is within yourself. In the desire for domestic harmony, you are resisting to the point of fatigue what appears to be inharmony. The stronger your emotional response to the inharmony, the greater will be your physical weariness. Do not waste your efforts in trying to change another. Direct all your mental and spiritual powers toward freedom for yourself. Speak your word along these lines: "I forgive everyone, even myself; no inharmonious element can obtain in my home. Everyone connected with this household is unified and identified in love, understanding, wisdom and illumination, and everyone is expressing his perfect part of the perfect Whole. I know there is a Divine Presence here, responding to my call, and I know I am that Presence."

When the old attitudes present themselves, refuse to recognize them. Silently say: "My real home is in Divine Mind, and my home is a haven of rest, a place of peace." Watch your emotions. Eternal vigilance, positively practiced, will heal the situation, and your work and your family will be a joy to you.

HANDLING PROBLEMS

Question—When one does not know how to handle a problem, how can one receive guidance?

ANSWER—To obtain the solution to any problem from within does not mean entering into a state of passivity. It does mean, however, doing a definite piece of scientific and spiritual work—clearing the mind of all adverse thought and being receptive to the Truth, speaking the word definitely, having unfailing faith in the Power of the Word. Thus are we in direct communion with God, *the All Good.* Here is a constructive method to follow. Declare daily: "Nothing but the true answer can present itself to me. I stand guard at the door of my conscious mind and nothing but that which I desire can enter. I know the solution to my problem is known in Infinite Mind and that Divine Intelligence within me directs and guides me."

A SUBNORMAL CHILD

Question—We are bringing a fourteen-year-old girl, whose mentality is seemingly retarded, into our home. Through an unfortunate circumstance she has been in a school for subnormal children. We wish to give her every advantage and would be grateful for suggestions for correct mental practice to help us work out this problem.

ANSWER—Not being concerned with evidence, we refute its claims absolutely and insist first that there never were any unfavorable circumstances that could retard anything. Second, all that is, is perfect, so the consciousness of this child is perfect; it is normal, natural and sustained by Infinite purposefulness. The need apparently is for all concerned to recognize this truth.

This truth specially spoken for (name of child) is the power and means of establishing for her that which in reality already is, Infinite Intelligence, and the normal activity of that Divine Idea which controls the universe is within her and is her very self in manifestation.

ATTAINING POISE

Question—How can perfect poise be attained so that one does and says the right thing at the right time?

ANSWER—Anything less than perfect adjustment will disturb that tremendous asset we call poise. It is within your power to say and do the right thing at all times. There is a perfect intelligence within you that guides and directs you, and a perfect law governing you always. Take the time each day for a meditation on this great Truth. Know within the depth of your own being that your conscious choosing mind is the controlling power. Say something like the following: "I know that the right word and the right act project themselves through me at the right time. Nothing can hinder my *word* from operating, and every situation in my life is handled with perfect peace and poise. I know that my word harmonizes into right action everything in my life, and that my word *is* Divine and there is nothing that can obstruct or hinder it from operating in and through all of my affairs. I am perfectly poised in this great Truth, and I am *always* master of any situation."

ABOLISHING SELF-PITY

Question—My sister has become estranged from me and as she is all that is left from our family, it grieves me very much. I seem to be walking in "the valley of the shadow." Although I have a good job, I almost go crazy for greater freedom and more companionship. How can I overcome this?

ANSWER—Self-pity can destroy every vestige of happiness for anyone; it has closed your eyes to the good all about you.

You alone are the arbiter of your reactions to external conditions. And to free yourself from this sense of loneliness you must give up all those little things that mar the day for you, and realize that you are created after the Image of Happiness, a finished Identity of the unseen side of your life, with every attribute that goes to make up Universal and Personal Love.

Love your sister more. Love everybody and your natural companions will be unable to resist your attraction. "To have a friend, be a friend." Seek to help someone who is lonely, and you will find yourself needed—and fulfilled. Do something for somebody else if you would find freedom and companionship. "Give love, and love to *your* life will flow," and God will companion you through some avenue of expression, perhaps unknown to you at the present time, for Love never faileth. It is the fulfilling of the law.

OVERCOMING HATRED TOWARD ANOTHER

Question—If one has been harboring a great hatred toward another, will it make his demonstration more possible if he confesses this and seeks forgiveness?

ANSWER—To seek forgiveness, one need turn toward no one but his inner Self, where he may unburden the unlovely attributes of his soul. He *knows* that in that inner fire of Love, all dross is burned up and only the pure gold remains. Two thoughts cannot occupy the same mind at the same time; neither can hatred and love occupy the same heart at the same time, and when hatred leaves, love will automatically take its place. However, if you have caused this person to feel your dislike, it might be well to take the matter up in your time of meditation. Tell your Indwelling all about it; ask to be given guidance and the words to heal the situation. You will get a lead, even though you are not conscious of its presence at the time. You will find the opportunity presents itself for you to make amends, and right words will be given you. But remember, love is a giver and not a getter. *Be very certain* that you are not subconsciously making a bargain with yourself. Your motive should be honestly and clearly examined and if the motive is for the sake of establishing God's harmony between yourself and your friend, it will prosper mightily and your demonstrations, all of which are fulfilled by love, cannot fail. We are warned against "Offering the body to be burned." It is the "Spirit that quickeneth."

NERVOUS DISORDER

Question—Please give advice for the following conditions: Nervous disorder of the stomach, depression, and discouragement.

ANSWER—To be rid of the above conditions, you must literally change your mind and you will change the cause. That which has been a source of chronic depression and discouragement must be neutralized by your refusal to allow it to register or affect you in the slightest. The nervous condition of the stomach is probably the result of lack of harmony and peace. Realize that the Spirit within you manifests as perfect harmony, and that every cell, atom, and organ of your body is functioning according to the Divine Law. Say: "I am filled with the peace, strength, and power of Spirit. The life forces flow freely, peacefully and harmoniously through every atom of my body, and I am complete and perfect now. The all-powerful Mind of the Indwelling Christ in me dissolves and dissipates from my mind all belief in depression and discouragement, for I dwell in the realm of Peace."

Set about to create through the power of your word, joyous, happy, and peaceful thoughts; and your nervous troubles will give place to the truth about yourself.

HELP FOR DOMESTIC INHARMONY

Question—Please advise me. My husband is ill-tempered, unreasonably jealous and insulting toward me, poisoning the children's minds. In the evening there are either apologies for the rudeness of the day before or the insults all over again. I never know which it will be. My health is telling the tale in loss of weight and strength.

ANSWER—Suppose you begin to think of your husband as the ideal man, rather than as being jealous and insulting. Perhaps the very suggestion of your thought and fear is operating through him. Assure your own mind that only that which is loving and kindly can come to you or be accepted by you, and you will soon find that the other condition will cease to be.

A BELIEF IN OLD AGE

Question—I seem to be too conscious of increasing years of physical life and too tired to do what I should do.

ANSWER—Being "too conscious" of the passage of years, with their burden of decreasing vitality, is the key to your problem. Life, activity, power and vitality do not decrease with the passage of years. Life, with all its color and tone, is as new today as it was the first day of the Divine Expression. Man, not understanding this truth, has seeded the great subconscious with a belief in old age and disability, and from this fertile field he harvests his experience. But within each individual there is that something which knows the truth, knows that there is no age, no incapacity; life already is, and always was. Freshen your mind and a renewal of the body must follow. Realize *what* you are, a *perfect idea in mind—without beginning or ending.* From the heart of this immutable Truth speak your word:

"Infinite Vitality within me, I behold Thee enthroned

in my temple of flesh. I feel Thy presence. I stand before Thee in joy and thanksgiving. I am sustained in strength by Thy life, which is ever active and fulfilling. Thy life flows through me now, and I am interested in my duties, which I dispatch with ease. My word, which is all-powerful, is a living thing, acting itself out in my experience.''

INDICATIONS OF HEALING

Question—In healing by mental and spiritual science, does one have aggravated symptoms at times as healing is taking place? It seems to me there would have to be some action or sensation physically.

ANSWER—Sometimes during the process of mental healing one has an aggravated symptom of the condition from which he has been suffering and sometimes old conditions come to the surface. This is called chemicalization and is a result of the uprooting of thought from the subjective side of life. Since it is the nature of thought to manifest, it often happens that when subjective thought habits are disturbed they produce an agitation both in mind and in body. In such a case, work should be done until a state of perfect normalcy results. It does not necessarily follow that there must always be a noticeable chemicalization; it is entirely possible for the healing to take place without any physical sensation whatever.

TREATMENT FOR BRONCHITIS

Question—Can you give me a good mental treatment for bronchitis? I can hardly speak without choking and coughing.

ANSWER—The treatment is simple and you should be able to effect your own healing by persistent mental practice. The first step is for you to recognize that far from being weak and helpless, you have only to choose and speak your word into that waiting substance which presses upon you at all times, and your word will act itself out according to that which you have declared unto it. Therefore speak with authority and be sure that you believe with all your soul that you have the power to heal yourself. Working thus, the congested thought which is centered in the bronchial tubes will be released: "I know that the Spirit of Infinite and Perfect Life is my life. I know that Absolute Intelligence controls every act of my life and that the purifying, energizing, unifying Life of God is now doing its perfect work in and through me; and I know that there is nothing in me to doubt or deny my word, and *I am free*—God's perfect idea, whole, sound, complete."

HABIT OF NOT SLEEPING

Question—I would like your opinion and advice for one who has forgotten how to sleep. I have no worries; it must be a habit, but I feel as though it would be a miracle if it were overcome.

ANSWER—If you are quite sure that your wakefulness is not due to subjective worry or anxiety, spend these night hours in constructive mental work. Ask the Infinite Indwelling Spirit of Peace to reveal to you the nature of the thing that is claiming the hours that should be spent in sleep. Work definitely and specifically for Peace, and declare, "I am right here and now in the Presence of God and in that Divine Presence there is no tension, no struggle, no fear. This Infinite Peace pours itself into my being and I am now relaxed in peace and sleep. The all-powerful Mind of the Indwelling Christ within me dissolves all sense of wakefulness and I am at peace." Do not, however, be disturbed about this condition; some of the world's best poets and writers have received their highest inspiration during the quiet hours of the night. But I am certain that you cannot successfully remain awake if your mental work is definite. Your word is all power and when it is linked to a living faith, there is nothing impossible to accomplish.

CHILDBIRTH

Question—What is the type of treatment to use in the case of childbirth?

ANSWER—Work for right action. In your treatment, realize that the great law of Creation is operative. Throw out all anxieties and fears, and unite yourself through your mind with the great unobstructed movement of Life as it projects into the objective world a new body. Dwell on the wonder of this knowing Intelligence which works out the entire scheme of a new body, imbuing it with its own laws of health and action, setting up the perfect working of the various systems, such as breathing, circulation, etc. Realize that your part is merely the full acceptance of the fact that the Creative Law within you knows, and not only knows but performs every action at the right time; that It synchronizes all impulses toward the advent. It is Its nature to do this. It could not do otherwise. Rest in the great peace of your mind and realize that Perfection is at work, forming and projecting into the objective world that upon which its action has been centered.

Let your meditation be somewhat as follows: "I am unified with Universal Law, creating, delivering, perfecting. I rest in my mind, rejoicing that I have only to accept the perfect results of this natural law. I give myself utterly to this perfect Law and am at peace. I am serene, because I know that I am in the care of Perfection in action."

TREATMENT OF TUMOR

Question—I have been seeking relief through Truth from an internal fibroid tumor. I work very hard on a ranch. I study until my head is weary, yet peace does not come. I want to work it out the right way, God's way. I want to stay on with my little son and husband. I have always been so fearful and now it seems self-pity is my trouble. Can you help me?

ANSWER—Perhaps in your treatment you have unconsciously held your condition to you by an over strenuous mental effort. It might be helpful for you to change this method of treatment and in your meditation simply state that you are now free from all burden or bondage and that the Spirit separates all false thought and manifestations from you. Seek to loose your thought and relieve the tension of your mind by a clear spiritual realization. Try consciously to let go of all your troubles and feel that they are disappearing from your experience. Those things which are not implanted by the Divine Spirit have no law to support them and dissolve in the intense light of spiritual recognition. This practice, I believe, will meet your problem.

CONTROL OF UNRULY CHILD

Question—My boy is very hard to manage. If he can tease or quarrel or be mean, he feels in his element.

ANSWER—Resistance is the keynote to this whole situation. The boy resists the Law and you are resisting his resistance. Place your son mentally in the center of Divine Consciousness and recognize that every negative quality is transmuted into a positive quality of good. Realize that your boy is a perfect individualized part of the perfect whole, that he is surrounded and permeated by the power of Love, which is invincible and fulfills all Law. Your work, done consciously, being stronger than his unconscious *misuse* of power, will bring about a change in his mental attitude. Keep your work secret and do not be discouraged if it takes a little time before results appear. Know that Love makes easy and desirable all activities toward the growth and development of every individual; therefore, he (your boy, naming him) is in perfect harmony with himself, with his schoolmates and with his home. Say: ''The Spirit of Love in him makes him kind. It softens and eradicates every hard attitude, for nothing unlike Itself can stand before Its transmuting power. My word is spoken for his freedom from all bondage and limitation, and I know there is nothing in him to hinder its perfect fulfillment.''

BUILDING BODILY STRENGTH

Question—I have been able to keep going, but am not equal to what is expected of a mother of four husky boys, on a farm. Can I be helped through mental treatment to build bodily strength?

ANSWER—The first step for you to take is to realize the truth about yourself. You have been seeing yourself as inadequate to the calls made on your physical strength by your family. See yourself strong, vital and radiantly equal to every need and circumstance. ''Know ye not that ye are the temple of the living God?'' This power within you is the same power that holds the planets in space. It is as efficacious in one place as in another. In your daily work realize that the Spirit of Infinite and Perfect Life is your life and that it is now manifesting through you as your strength and vitality. See yourself strong because of this indwelling strength.

Words similar to these will prove effective and sure: ''I know that the Spirit of Life within me is my vitality and strength and I feel the power of life, vitality, strength and joy flowing through me now. I know the power back of my word is perfect law and is fulfilled and returned to me as my perfect strength. I am adequate to every call.''

IMPEDIMENT OF SPEECH

Question—Please tell me what treatment to use for my little son, whose speech is defective. He is in an institution. I have not seen him since last November and I am discouraged and sad.

ANSWER—Being discouraged and sad yourself focuses a mental discouragement and sadness into the whole situation, and will have a retarding effect in your son's progress. Rather, be grateful that he is in a place where he has the constant ministrations and training of persons who are specialists in their work. Realize, *"one with God* is a totality,'' and nothing is impossible to the all-loving Mind of God in which your child lives and moves and has his being. Use a treatment like this daily: Clear the mind of all fear and worry and see your son as being happy, whole, complete; a normal boy in every way. Know that the Life which is God flows through him and heals and vitalizes every organ of his body. Know that there is no impediment of speech in Divine Mind, and know that the Spirit of Infinite and Perfect Life is his life, that absolute Intelligence controls every act of his life, and that he is the all-loving, all-conquering son of God, fearless and free.

DAILY SPEAKING THE WORD

Question—Should one continually speak the word, each day, for that which he is asking, or is it only necessary to say it one or two days and then wait for the fulfillment of the word?

ANSWER—Yes, one should not only speak the word each day, but he should meditate on the fact that the word is a living thing endowed with the power and intelligence to act itself out as the condition he wishes to see manifest. Such meditation is analogous to watering the seed you plant in your garden. This daily spoken word causes the impression to sink deeper and deeper into the creative soil of the subjective; and you should be careful to introduce no element that would tend to alter or neutralize the word. All outlining should be left to the Indwelling Intelligence which knows just how to fulfill.

"The definite, persistent, scientific repetition of the same idea in the same Mind, brings the awakening in the form of demonstration."

OVERCOMING SELF-CONSCIOUSNESS

Question—How can I overcome self-consciousness and an inferiority complex?

ANSWER—You suffer because you are directing your mental forces toward that which is not the *real you*. The treatment lies in realizing what *you* really are. You are that splendid, radiant, all-conquering Son of God—the capable exponent of Life Itself, and you are as necessary to this Infinite Expression as Life is necessary to your experience. The Spirit in the person before whom you quail is the very same Spirit that is within you, for Spirit is One. Why tremble before yourself? These qualities which you admire in another, self-assurance and charm, are elements in your own make-up. If this were not so, you could not know them, since we only know that which we are. The treatment lies in reversing your mental process. Realize that whatever good you recognize in another is part of yourself. Say, as the ancients taught their pupils to say, "Wonderful, wonderful, wonderful me." Realize that this "me" is holy, divine substance and life, known in Mind by your own name, and do not violate your own peace by separating yourself from your indwelling Christ. A persistent practice of this realization will heal anyone of negative self-consciousness and will energize and vitalize the true positive Self-Consciousness.

THE DRINK HABIT

Question—How shall I treat one who is an alcoholic?

ANSWER—The spirit within this man is the answer. The spirit of man is the Spirit of God, and it cannot long for anything. There is nothing in him that feels incomplete or inferior. His whole being is satisfied. He has both a conscious and subjective knowledge of reality. He feels equal to any and every situation, and knows that he does not have to take any stimulant of any nature whatsoever to give him satisfaction or to produce happiness. He is conscious that he is happy in his own right, complete and perfect in his own being, divine and whole right now. There is no lure nor imagination, no enticement, no suggestion in the thought of alcohol or false stimulants. They are neither person, place nor thing, have no law of their own, are absolutely non-intelligent, and cannot assail this man's imagination nor cross his mind. There is no subjective and no objective habit of alcoholism. The spirit within this man is radiant. It does not remember ever having had any desire to drink. It cannot contemplate any such desire. It is forever removed from any such desire. This man is not poisoning his own thought and his own life; he is happy and complete in his own consciousness; he is now free and will forever remain free.

A NORMAL CHILD

Question—I am asking you to help me to solve a problem which I have been trying to solve for the past few years. It is in reference to my son, who is now the age to get out in the business world, but somehow something has held him back mentally all these years. As it is every mother's desire to have her child normal in every way, I ask your help.

ANSWER—You state rather positively that "something has held him back mentally." Whatever the stumbling block has been, it appears to have been accepted by your mind as a real impediment. The truth about your boy is that he is a perfect idea in the great Universal Harmony, and as such he is active, progressive, mentally alert and responsive.

The thing for you to do is to declare the truth about him *to yourself.* You must wipe out the mental picture you have carried "all these years" if you really want him to take his place in the world.

Know without a shadow of doubt that all the mental keenness there is, is an active faculty of his mind. Know that Divine Mind knows him as an active, successful, progressive part of Itself, and that It compels him to think, say and do the right thing at the right time.

ACQUIRING SELF-CONFIDENCE

Question—I am a good bookkeeper, capable of installing systems in all branches, and with it all I am a miserable coward, afraid of my own shadow because I can't see a pay check ahead of me the first and fifteenth of each month. Can this fear be overcome?

ANSWER—Realize once and for all that the Intelligence within you is not and never could be afraid. There is nothing other than this Intelligence—It directs and guides you and for It to be afraid of anything, It would have to fear Itself. There is only one tool with which to chisel out the effect you desire—that is your *word*, and within your word lies everything necessary for it to become the condition or circumstance you wish to see manifested.

Form the treatment in your own words to this effect and *feel* the Truth of them as you speak them: "Within me is *invincible* Intelligence. I know that I am guided by this Intelligence. I am equipped for expression and there is nothing in the way of my fulfillment—no doubt—no anxiety—no fear. *My opportunity finds me* and there can be no delay. My place is in Divine Mind and I know it. My consciousness comprehends enough of the Infinite to bring my success and fulfillment into manifestation now.''

TREATMENT FOR RIGHT ADJUSTMENT

Question—I have worked in different lines, but always unsuccessfully. Can you help me find my right work here and now, the work for which I am best fitted and in which I will make a success?

ANSWER—Suppose we go farther into mind than merely finding your chosen work, ''here and now,'' and see if we can find *you*. After we have found out *what* you are, we will then find out what you really want to do. This finding of yourself is the base from which all right action comes.

In and by the One Mind you are known as a Point of Consciousness; therefore, you have the power to *know* whatever you choose to know. Your knowing is done with and in this One Mind, since there is no other mind. Consequently, you and this Mind are One and the same thing. That is *what you are.*

Since this One Mind knows all things, together with ways and means of projecting them into your experience, your mental work lies in recognizing that this Mind knows, within your consciousness, just what line of business you should follow in order to achieve the particular success you want.

Give yourself this scientific treatment and repeat it until you know what you want to do:

''Since this Mind is everywhere, It is within me; It knows everything; therefore, I realize that It knows my right business activity. Being One with It, I know now, with this inner Knower, what I am best fitted for. My success is assured because my way is opened by this Knower, which is also the only Actor—I rest easy in anticipation, sure of my good.''

This treatment, repeated often enough, will result in the disclosure in your consciousness of the right path for you to follow. Be courageous and follow it without hesitation. This method will open channels and avenues through which your good flows, and you will draw to yourself the very thing that is best.

THE PROCESS OF HEALING

Question—Please explain the process of healing, as it is accomplished by a practitioner for a patient. One can easily accept the idea of an individual receiving help through making his own contact, but how a third person can do more than just assist the patient by stimulating his own faith is rather vague.

ANSWER—The process of mental healing is one of mentally knowing that the one being helped is now Perfect. There is but one Mind in the universe and all are in this Mind. When you know the truth within this Mind you are knowing it within the mind of your patient—if he is receptive to the Truth.

The practitioner does not hold a thought, nor does he send out a thought. He thinks the Truth, leaving the result to the action of the Law.

FEAR OF ACCIDENTS

Question—My wife has just been through two serious accidents, one an auto accident and one a fall from which she received a crushed elbow. She is absolutely consumed with fear of something else happening to her. Can you suggest how to help her combat her sense of fear?

ANSWER—It is easy to sense the old superstition, "If one accident occurs there will surely be three," at work here. There is no more power in this old idea than we give to it. Of course, if you definitely expect the third one, it will come to you. That is the way the law works. But if you definitely know that two accidents are aplenty and that you neither expect nor accept another because "accidents" do not belong to you, you will free yourself of the old subtle race belief which delivered the second accident to you. Neutralize the fear of accidents by knowing there are no accidents in Divine Mind. Speak your word for Divine protection. You are one with the Originating Spirit and your word has power. Stop fearing by knowing and practicing faith in your good.

PAIN UNBEARABLE

Question—Please advise what to do. I have either acute stomach trouble or gallstones. Some say one thing and others another. All I can say is the pain is almost unbearable, whether I am lying down or sitting up. Sleep is impossible.

ANSWER—From the nature of this question it appears that the writer has a definite condition to meet and this condition should either be met on the mental or the physical plane. It is a great mistake for a student of the Truth to say that nothing ails him while he is suffering either mentally or physically. If one can meet the condition through right mental treatment then he has demonstrated on that plane. If, however, he is unable to do this or to have it done for him successfully, he should not say that everything is right when it is wrong. This is self-deception, which is neither sense or science. The demonstration of the Science of Mind and the power of spiritual thought-force over material resistance is not a process of hypnotism, but when successfully used produces an actual physical change, and unless this *physical* change takes place there is no demonstration. The writer of this question should either make his demonstration through mental and spiritual treatment or he should seek help on the physical plane from those competent to advise him.

MATERIAL REMEDIES

Question—If you are treating yourself for health and seem to respond rather slowly, is it unscientific in the meantime to resort to material remedies?

ANSWER—It is scientific to use every measure that is necessary to improve the condition. The unscientific thing is to quarrel mentally with the measures you find necessary to use. You should have no thought of conflict between what we call the spiritual method and the material, for in truth there is but the One Health, and health is both spiritual and material. In the last analysis, the material is but a visible vibration of the Spirit and the life that is Spirit permeates every living thing. The unscientific trend of thought will establish a conflict between Spirit and matter if full realization of their oneness is not definite in your mind. "Both the Absolute and the relative are reflected in the mirror of matter." Do not try to go beyond your understanding. Our understanding is not sufficient to enable us to set bones, and since we cannot walk on the water, we take a boat. We can go only as far as we know. Principle is Infinite, but we can demonstrate only at the level of our own concept. There is nothing wrong in any method of treatment providing it relieves suffering, but lest the suffering come again the mental *cause* must be removed.

PHYSICAL VISION

Question—Should I take off my glasses before I am conscious of an improvement in my physical vision?

ANSWER—We never reap the harvest until we have consciously planted the seed. Nor do we plant until the soil is carefully prepared.

If your intuition has given you the promise that you can get along without your glasses, and you are sure it was the Voice of your Indwelling Perfection, you may throw them away and go your way rejoicing. But if you are merely experimenting to see if you no longer need them, you are not yet on the positive side of your problem and would better continue wearing them. When you feel that they are not needed, with an assurance that brooks no shadow of conjecture or doubt, you are healed. When that moment comes, you will be unable to use them. For example, consider the episode of Jesus and Peter walking on the water. Jesus really *knew* that natural laws obeyed him, while Peter was in that state of realization where old doubts could assail him. Consequently Jesus walked safely while Peter sank.

NO PHYSICAL SENSATION IN TREATMENT

Question—By what evidence shall we know *that we* really do *contact Universal Mind—that is, the highest point of the subjective mind touching the lowest point of the Infinite? Does it bring any physical sensation?*

ANSWER—A physical sensation is not necessary to the demonstrating of Truth, any more than a physical sensation is necessary to the knowledge that two and two make four.

We know that we know, when we can no longer ask the question as to whether or not we do know.

The subjective mind is the medium between the Absolute and the relative and the tendency of the subjective mind decides what is to happen to us.

All mental healing is to clarify the mind within and without and cause it to be receptive to that Life which is already perfect.

However, there is a definite sense of completion when a good treatment is given.

OVERCOMING RESENTMENT

Question—If only I could overcome a feeling of resentment which takes possession of me. I live in an atmosphere of constant criticism and intolerance. For a while I can smile through it all and then, all of a sudden, it seems so unjust I can't stand any more and negative emotions take possession of me.

ANSWER—Those with whom you live may have permitted these unlovely habits to fasten themselves on them and to color their action, but if you would be unaffected by this atmosphere you must transcend it. Do not even be affected to the point of seeing the necessity to "smile through it all." Consciously smiling through that which you subconsciously concede to be a trying circumstance is fostering conflict. It is like clamping the lid on danger. Blowing the lid off is the natural consequence. Enduring what we cannot cure is not the way to demonstrate. Behind everything there is only the *One*. Resolve the whole discordant situation into that and proceed to get the right reaction. No one can possibly hurt you if you yourself refuse to be hurt. Reveal the Truth to yourself—that there is no discord—no inharmony—no misunderstanding here. That which is the Truth must be perfect. Our method is to transcend conditions and to know that there is only the One Mind and that there is no misunderstanding, no resistance, no resentment in the One Mind. Thus can all belief in separation be neutralized, and to the degree that you do this will you be free from all sense of criticism and intolerance. Peace always neutralizes discord. Treat for peace and poise and try to sense that Love unifies with reality and finds itself to be One. *Love more* and look to your own reactions. When you can honestly say, "None of these things move me" you will have freed yourself from the entire plane of antagonism. Be ever alert and awake and declare daily that, "My word dissolves all discord and resentment. I am conscious of only that which is peaceful and harmonious. The pathway of peace is everlasting unfoldment."

TRIANGLE CASE DISTRESSES

Question—Please help me or tell me how to help myself. Three years ago my husband left me for another woman. After a time he came back and I thought he was sincere in returning, but he is cold and cruelly indifferent. I have learned that he is corresponding with the other woman and sending her money and gifts. I have tried to live one day at a time, holding to the faith that my husband would come back to me. Can you help me?

ANSWER—In the Truth we learn this: that which is not ours we cannot hold and that which is ours we cannot help holding. You have no right nor should you seek to coerce your husband, nor is it scientific treatment to make any attempt to cause him to come back to you. Set him free in your own mind and know that whatever is for his best good and yours will be done. Try to heal yourself of the belief that your happiness depends upon anything outside of your own consciousness. If you do this you will attract friendship and love into your life far beyond your fondest hopes.

CAN ONE RELY ON GOD?

Question—I am in need of healing for many things. Can you tell me how, and is it really a sure fact, that one can rely on God, or Divine Life, for health? Will you explain this to me?

ANSWER—It is proven that a complete reliance on God can bring about definite results. This reliance is not a blind belief but is a scientific approach to Reality through the creative power of the mind. Spiritual healing is the result of correct mental knowing. The only approach to Reality that we have is through our thought, belief and receptivity to Life.

To sense one's being as divine is scientific and will work wonders. To completely control the thought and constantly direct all its activities along constructive channels will heal the body.

To scientifically rely on God is practical as well as idealistic. God is the Life Energy and the Intelligent Principle running through everything. God is in you. Realize this indwelling God as the One and only Life.

CONTROL OF WORRY

Question—I am the best little worrier you ever saw and drive my husband frantic worrying about things that never happen. Is there a permanent cure for this?

ANSWER—There is indeed a permanent cure. Realize within yourself that God did not create fear. Its opposite, Peace, is God's creation. Fear is the greatest bogeyman in the race belief, and out of it comes every sickness and inharmonious condition known to man. Its companion is ignorance, and where we find one we are very apt to find the other. Fear is the arch enemy of man and it must be absolutely destroyed before there is any possibility of letting in the light. This enemy must be eliminated—*expelled forever.* In your daily meditation use this treatment: "I am filled with the peace of heaven. There is nothing in God's perfect Creation but perfect Peace and there is nothing to fear. Nothing but thoughts of peace and faith and courage can enter my conscious mind, for I do not recognize anything but peace. I am free, spiritually and mentally free—fearless and free."

UNIFYING WITH ALL GOOD

Question—In claiming Infinite supply and that all channels are open through which I may receive good, would I automatically close any channel by denying my dependence upon one individual or business?

ANSWER—In claiming Infinite supply, it is unnecessary to deny anything. In making such a claim one automatically accepts all the good that Universal supply has for him. The avenues and channels are part and parcel of the claim. Individuals, personalities, conditions, etc., are not considered at all, because it is on the Absolute or undifferentiated Spirit you are calling. The only thing you have to do is to recognize the spiritual truth that your good is present, pressing upon you and through you for expression, and that you determine, by your choice, the form this good is to take. Denying your dependence on personality or condition is a subtle admission of the dependence you would deny.

A conscious unity with the All-good within you will make you so positive, so sure of the Presence of supply for every need, that you will have no room to mentally entertain a possible opposing force. The thing to work for is Unity.

To learn how to think is to learn how to live, for our thoughts go into a Medium that is Infinite in Its ability to do and to be. Man, by thinking, can bring into his experience whatsoever he desires, if he thinks correctly and becomes a living embodiment of his thoughts.

Treat yourself to see no separation between yourself and the All-good. Know that the All-good is present in its entirety within you. Claim its manifestation in your experience and affairs, and *know it will happen for you as you have spoken and believed.*

DISPELLING LONELINESS

Question—Can you help me solve the problem of loneliness, and of finding my happiness?

ANSWER—Be firm and change your reactions to life. Since life takes us at our own valuation, it gives back to us exactly as we give to it. If your world is one of loneliness, you must change this subjective impression—you must furnish the pattern. Quietly and calmly, try to feel, to sense the joy of friendliness within you—love more. Feel love for people welling up within you and you will find this magnetic vibration will entirely change your outlook on life. If you do this, you will be so charged with the power of attraction that nothing and nobody can resist your friendship. Take time daily to feel the God within you expressing Itself as happiness and peace and joy.

Say something like this: "I am filled with love. My life is rich and full and abundant. I love everybody and see in everyone the perfect manifestation of love *and that love responds to me*. Love through me fulfills my desire and brings me happiness and friends."

HEALED THROUGH PRAYER

Question—I have been ill for a number of years and wish to know how to become healed through prayer.

ANSWER—There is a point of stillness within every person's mind where he may become actively aware of the presence of life. Spend as much of your time as is possible in this "Place of Peace," just knowing that you are the perfect child of God. When you have so impressed your subjective mind with peace that you are cognizant of nothing other, then go a step further and speak your word for perfect health of mind, body and affairs. We know that our thought lays hold of Causation and manipulates real Substance. We know that the word of man is the law of his life, under the One Great Law of all Life. We know that a realization of the presence of God is the most powerful healing agency known to the mind of man. We know that we can heal to the degree that we can think from the higher motive; and we know that we should be constantly on the alert, seeking to embody higher thoughts.

For your healing, then, find that place of peace within you and when you actually feel that blessed freedom from all worldly concern, realize that you are, *that instant*, at home with God, the loving Father. And ask Him for an abiding consciousness of His Presence as your mental and physical health. Daily practice will release you into a divine realization of your unity with the All Good.

PROBLEM OF HARMONY

Question—What must I do to establish harmony? My son was married before he had finished school. I am trying to help him but his wife is inclined to be jealous. If the fault is mine, I want to know and overcome it.

ANSWER—In treating, know that Love is stronger than any other force in the Universe and that It flows through this situation and cleanses it from all misunderstanding. Realize in your own mind that jealousy can have no place in your own experience. As you confine your treatment to your own experience and declare for perfect harmony, you are working on the plane of First Cause. Realize very definitely there is nothing in your life but love (because you will admit of nothing else). Know it persistently and love will become apparent in the attitude of those who contribute to your life of daily experiences. Harmonize your own thinking and declare that, "There is no misunderstanding, resistance to the Truth, resentment or jealousy in Divine Mind. There is but the one perfect peace and harmony flowing in and through each and every one of us, and I know that there is no presence other than the perfect Mind and that in this Mind and Spirit I am free, happy, joyous and at peace."

PREVENTING REGRETS

Question—How can one prevent the mind from feeling regrets, and from running in circles, resulting in loss of appetite and upset stomach?

ANSWER—It is the emotional nature that feels regret. Take yourself in hand and center your mental energy on Peace. Realize that there is One Infinite Mind which is consciously directing your destiny, and whatever the nature of your "regret" may be, declare that there are no mistakes in Infinite Mind and that there is no memory of yesterday other than the memory of peace and joy, and no anticipation of tomorrow other than one of peace and poise and joy. Direct your attention in the opposite direction. No practice is more futile than that of whipping the thought in a circle around a situation that does not exist, except in memory—and memory presents to you but a picture. Say: "The Lord, my God, within the midst of me *is* peace, and I am filled with tranquillity. There is nothing in the universe which can cause me to be disturbed. I have no regrets for I am peace."

Do this until you have proved its truth.

NEUTRALIZING NEGATIVE MENTAL ATTITUDES

Question—I am a graduate nurse, but have grown weary of so much night duty and being constantly in a sick atmosphere. I have become negative and have no work. I still want to be active. I realize that I have drifted into a wrong and negative mental attitude, so I am asking for help to overcome this conditon.

ANSWER—The work for you in treating should be centered around the thought of right activity, realizing that there is no obstruction to right action. In your daily meditation, keep the thought-current focused on the truth that right activity for you is an established fact in Mind; that there is nothing between you and this activity but your thought; and that your Word now spoken for this specific purpose clears your path of all obstruction and frees you. Realize that in truth you are never in a sick atmosphere, for there is no such thing in Divine Mind. Realize that your services soothe, lift and bless those persons who labor under false beliefs and experiences, and that nothing can, or wants to, hinder your services in this ministry.

HEREDITARY TENDENCIES

Question—My child, twelve years old, seems anemic. I have a consciousness of hereditary tendencies, since tuberculosis has been in the family. Could my thought affect him? Can we transcend heredity?

ANSWER—Yes, decidedly we can transcend heredity. Fear for your child in your own mind will communicate itself to his mind and should it become a fixation, he would probably manifest the weaknesses which you recognize as hereditary tendencies. A strong, positive mental attitude toward health for him, dropping and forgetting all thoughts of heredity, knowing that he is an individual of the new order, immune to diseases of the past which your family have suffered, will work wonders in your child.

Know within yourself that your child is really not your child at all, but the child of *perfect Life* under a *perfect Law* and performing or manifesting in *perfect Action,* which is health. Talk to him, think it for him and for yourself, and talk and think nothing contrary and you will find he will be well. Know that your boy is God's perfect child—whole, sound, perfect, complete and sustained in the One Infinite Mind—God.

ACQUIRING RECEPTIVITY

Question—We have a poultry ranch. We love our home; we like the work and everything about it except the sum we still owe on the ranch. I know God has that somewhere for us, but why don't we receive it? I am also in need of healing. I believe God has health, happiness and wealth in abundance for us all and for me, and wants to give it to us and to me. Now what am I to do to receive it?

ANSWER—The Spirit can only give us what we can take, and since the taking is a mental process, it is necessary for you to accept the fact that the Spirit has already provided the means for you to discharge all of your obligations. In your treatment, work to convince your own mind that this has already taken place, *resolutely turning from every attempt to see how it might take place* and completely accept that it is already done. The answer to prayer is in the prayer when it is prayed and unless it is, there will be no answer. Mental treatment is for the purpose of convincing one's own mind, since the Eternal Mind is already convinced. When our individual minds unqualifiedly accept the action of the Universal Mind in us and through us and for us, we demonstrate the Truth and find ourselves healed and surrounded by abundance.

REALIZING PROSPERITY

Question—I just cannot bring myself to realize prosperity. I was brought up in a home that never knew a great deal of abundance, and my early religious training tended to cause me to doubt and suspect God and to accept lack as His will. This makes it very difficult for me to accept as my own the things I desire, which I know God, or the Infinite Intelligence, is offering me. How can I make myself realize that with God all things are possible; that prosperity is here and everywhere and that I can demonstrate it for myself?

ANSWER—The answer to your question is the answer to the whole apparent enigma of life: "How may we become reconciled to and unified with Reality, for within Reality is abundance as well as peace and happiness?" The gradual dawning of a sense of one's unity with the Whole involves a process of time and we should be satisfied if our tendency is in the right direction. Do not try to force things, but rather in the quiet contemplation of your own thought, seek to sense the Divine Presence, not only as a reality but as an availability. In the quietude of this mental receptivity to the spirit of life, seek to sense that it is surrounding you with everything necessary to your happiness and to your success. And then as you let go of this concept become expectantly receptive to its fulfillment.

PART IV

Authority Over Conditions

HOW TO CHANGE

Question—My work takes me into an extremely material thinking environment. I would like your advice in treating for harmony and understanding—then for a change of environment.

ANSWER—To be free *from* any situation, it is necessary to be free *in* it. By this we mean that it must be handled in mind in such a way that a positive attitude is evolved and brought to bear upon it.

To establish yourself in a positive attitude necessitates a constant, conscious exercise of poise. Realize that there is within you and within your environment a point where perfect peace prevails at all times; that no contrary manifestation reaches or disturbs this calm power. Withdraw from the outward appearance and consciously contact this place of power and peace. Do this often during the day. It may be difficult when you first begin, but by making the attempt repeatedly you will succeed in becoming conscious of it. Declare that your good governs you, your circumstances and your environment. Decide in your own mind that this is true and do not waver. Your good will come to you in this situation or you will have an opportunity to make the change you desire. When you know that good governs, and you expect a manifestation of that government, nothing but good can touch your life.

MEETING OBLIGATIONS

Question—My husband is fine, honorable and loving, but without a background of belief in orthodox religion. He has been trying to apply New Thought principles, but suffers from fear, anxiety and worry. He has too little confidence in himself to drive a car, which is a handicap in his business. We have considerable excellent vacant property which we cannot sell to meet our honest obligations, something we have always met. How may we demonstrate freedom from these limitations?

ANSWER—I should work to know that everything in my life and affairs is controlled by Divine Intelligence. By this I mean to take a definite time every day to declare that the Spirit of Intelligence is guiding and controlling everything in my life, meeting all my needs and supplying every desire which is legitimate. I should not worry about my husband's religion but leave him intellectually and spiritually free. We are all individuals and each must light his own particular path to the City of Perfection.

LAW OF NON-RESISTANCE

Question—Is the law of non-resistance the law to use when caught in undesirable business relations?

ANSWER—We must understand that non-resistance does not mean saying everything is all right when it is all wrong. It is the non-recognition of the reality and the vitality of the wrong; non-resistance to it as an entity and the active, conscious and aggressive recognition of the right. It is denial of the error and affirmation of the truth. We should not just sit down and say it is right if it is wrong, but we should know that the wrong has no power and the right is manifest.

TREATING FOR RIGHT ACTION

Question—How can we obtain what we desire?

ANSWER—It would not be a good thing if we could always have what we wish for. This is not a true idea of prayer. True prayer is always "Thy will be done." But the reaction to this prayer is not morbid. It is not in accord with divine will that we be unhappy, sick, poor, afraid. Whatever the Divine will is, it must be peace, joy, goodness, abundance, happiness, spontaneity, wholeness, opulence, success. Scientific prayer or treatment works for things in their original sense and lets them flow into experience along the line of least resistance, which is the way all natural forces work. "Thy will" is a prayer that the God-will, the Cosmic will, is expressed in its completeness, hence there is no limit to such a prayer. One would pray for abundance, physical healing, etc., knowing that he is in line with the Divine will, but he would not pray that everything he wished might happen, because in our present state of evolution we are not wise enough to always know what is best.

PURSUING THE RIGHT COURSE

Question—How can one be sure he is pursuing the right course in his quest for happiness and success?

ANSWER—One should treat to know that that which makes for his greatest success and most complete happiness is now in his experience. Look always to the idea, never to the way in which it is going to manifest. But if things begin to happen pointing toward a way, deliberately work to know that if this is best, the way will open. If one is not sure what to do and there appear to be many things that could be done, he should treat to realize that the Indwelling Intelligence knows what to do and compels him into right action.

MAKING THINGS "CLICK"

Question—Both my husband and son have demonstrated their ability in the past, but at present nothing seems to "click." Can you help us in the present emergency?

ANSWER—Since the Divine plan is immutable, enduring forever, unfolding just as rapidly as man will allow it to unfold, it follows that whatever man may think and do must be done within the body of this plan. Success in the past? There is no past—there is *always* the everlasting now. *Today* we enter into the full consciousness of abundance. Let go of the picture that makes you compare the "past" with the "present." Infinite Intelligence, alive and aware in your husband and son, is just as potent today as at any time. Your spoken word thrown into universal subjectivity for their prosperity and activity will set forces in motion that cannot be denied—your word contains within itself all of the elements necessary to its fulfillment and *it will not return "void."*

Speak words like these into Mind daily: "I know that this word for prosperity which I speak is Life and Law and Power. I know that there is no presence other than the Perfect Mind and Spirit and that my success is assured right here and now."

CHANGING UNPLEASANT SURROUNDINGS

Question—Does indifference to unpleasant surroundings change them for the better?

ANSWER—This would be saying peace when there is no peace. And this is what we must be careful to avoid. While indifference to unpleasant surroundings might make them more bearable, the mind should exercise an active and a progressive campaign to neutralize them and to create pleasant ones.

AGE LIMIT IN BUSINESS

Question—I have no business and no employment. I have sought diligently for weeks but everywhere have been met with the age limitation (my age being 53 years) and also with the bond requirements and other conditions which I could not meet. How can I solve this problem?

ANSWER—Formulate your treatment so as to make it independent of the belief in age or of any other condition. The treatment should be the thing since it is the cause of that which is to be created. Place absolute reliance upon your treatment and let it be free from any sense of limitation. Allow the treatment to be an absolute entity in the mental world. Speak it into consciousness with the full expectancy that it will accomplish and with a complete receptivity to the result which your mind now agrees will be forthcoming.

HEATED ARGUMENT

Question—I live in a very chaotic environment—among argumentative people. My refusal to get into heated arguments with them brings down their disapproval on my head and I find myself becoming angry at their condemnation and hating them. How can I treat myself?

ANSWER—Anger is an aspect of resistance. As long as anger can force a reaction through you, their inharmony is really active within your own subjective, though it does not show itself in your conscious mind until your position of independence is attacked. Then, what you have been listening to and witnessing comes forth as resentment against their attitude toward you. You have nothing to defend and therefore should not be on the defensive. Treat yourself to know that your calm has nothing to do with anyone except yourself; that it is a part of your being, balanced, sane, and independent of anything anyone may do or say in your presence.

FINDING THE RIGHT WORK

Question—I have an objective as to what I want to be, but I cannot form a definite objective of what I ought to do. I have a multitude of things before me I might try to do, but cannot settle on the one thing I should do. How can I overcome this confusion?

ANSWER—Since you cannot choose one activity from the others, give the problem to Mind. Say something like this— "I know that the Divine Intelligence within me knows what the particular work is for me to do. It knows the right activity to bring about my objective. I rely on it to open the way; to show me the sign that points out the right action. I realize this Divine guidance is within me *now,* and that activity works through me and cannot be withheld from my affairs." Then watch for the sign. "Listen greatly to yourself." Often the harvest of the seed we have sown is borne to us from most unexpected sources. Your word thus spoken deals with the perfect law and this law guides, directs and governs you, and is liberty and freedom, success and happiness unto you.

THERE ARE NO SETBACKS

Question—After experiencing much help from mental work, my husband's business seemed to go backward again. We were so happy and hopeful, please tell us the cause of this change in condition.

ANSWER—Treat to know that there can be no backward steps, no reversal of constructive conditions and nothing in you to believe in any. Reaffirm the truth and reestablish all the peace you have ever experienced as being a continuous activity in your life. Know that the word which you speak is the Truth and that there is nothing in you which can hinder it from operating.

COMPETITION

Question—How would you handle the idea of poor business? When the volume of business in a certain line is limited and there are several companies after it, how do you dispose of the reality of competition?

ANSWER—We would handle the idea of poor business through the counter realization that the Divine Mind is ever operating in your affairs and that there can be no inaction in this Mind. If our thought rises to the place where we perceive that there is no competition and no monopoly, it will either prove to us, in our immediate business, that we have no competitors whom we need to fear, or the result will be that we shall be brought into some field of action where there will be no need to think of competition.

RAISE OF SALARY

Question—I would like to know if it is right for me to use your mental treatment methods for a raise in my husband's salary. He likes his work but puts in long hours and the salary is very small. We are grateful for it but feel we need more supply, as we are in debt and cannot pay our bills on the present salary. We would greatly appreciate learning how to improve our thought so we can meet this situation.

ANSWER—I would treat directly to know that both you and your husband are surrounded by opportunities for self-expression and that every need in your life is met through the law of abundance, looking not to the source but to the idea. There is an inherent power in true ideas which causes them to take form in the objective world and become a part of the experience of everyday life. Your belief in and receptivity to this inherent power definitely embodied in your ideas will find an outlet.

AVENUES OF OPPORTUNITY

Question—An opportunity has been offered me which at first appeared to be perfect in every respect. Now I am put off and put off but always enough encouragement and assurance are given me to keep me interested. Should I turn from that to something else or stick with it as long as there is any hope?

ANSWER—Go within yourself and find out if this opportunity is really what you want. Ask the universal subjective mind within you to reveal to you the truth about the situation, *expect* the truth to come forth, and allow your mind to recognize it when it does appear in your conscious mind. It is a good practice to affirm daily: "There is no want of knowledge; I know the truth about this condition, for God is Truth and I instantly know all that I need to know about it." Realize that you cannot make such a demand and not have it answered. For that which you are addressing can do no other than obey you. And know that the Intelligence to which you address yourself is Truth Itself. Stay with this One and never deviate from It; never leave It for a moment. Nothing else can equal this attitude. Wait till you see results in your conscious mind before stopping the work. But know that you must have your answer, and be ever on the alert to receive and act upon it. Other avenues may present themselves in the meantime for your objective activity. If they do, take them by all means, but do not give up the idea that you can know the truth about the opportunity you mention. If it is really yours, you may have it. In fact, you cannot be kept out of it. What is yours is part and parcel of you.

HARMONY IN THE HOME

Question—Please help me to establish harmony in our home.

ANSWER—Every idea must stand on its own feet. If you

treat yourself directly to know that there is no interference in your personal affairs, you will find that all attempts at such interference will be dissolved. This treatment can be applied in your case. Meditate as follows:

"My home life is a harmony of joy, love and trust. There is nothing to interfere with the even flow of love in and through it." Contemplate it as you would have it, and *see no other mental picture.* Persistent knowing of the truth that "there is no interference in your personal affairs," believing it with all your soul in the very face of apparent contradiction, will win the day for you.

THE ART OF MAKING FRIENDS

Question—I sincerely love people. I make every possible gesture of friendship. I long so greatly for friends, but I never seem to make any.

ANSWER—Love begets love. We have learned this through experience. A recognition that the other person is but another Embodiment of the Great Self, even as you yourself are an Embodiment of that Universal One, will smooth out all difficulties that present themselves. Being of the essence and substance of the Great Whole, there should be a distinct realization that the Great Indivisibility is personalized in you. You are a vivid factor of Its expression, but you can never be divided or separated from It. Therefore, these other individuals that you say you love must of necessity love you.

Keep on loving people, but more than anything else, keep on loving that great fundamental principle of life which makes us all One. There need never be a sense of loneliness, of apartness, of being unloved. Your very exercise of the love-urge—in giving to others the affection you would like to experience yourself from others—will eventually bring you the particular personal satisfaction you crave.

MAKING CORRECT DECISIONS

Question—Two opportunities for activity are presented to me and they are equally attractive; will you please give me some idea how to work for guidance toward making the best choice?

ANSWER—Assume a positive mental attitude of dependence upon Infinite Intelligence. Know that this Infinite Intelligence, being all-wise, can only make correct decisions. Realize that this Infinite Intelligence is the only intelligence that can operate through you; since this is the case, you yourself need not assume the responsibility of trying to make a decision.

In treating, know: "Infinite Intelligence, God's Intelligence, now operating in and through me as my intelligence, makes right decisions only and has already made them in my behalf. I rest in peace knowing that my problem is solved."

A SALESMAN'S QUESTION

Question—I am a salesman—with one of the best companies in its line—prices, quality and service are right. When I have a well-to-do prospect who knows my company, admits that he needs my goods and has the money to pay for them, and yet hesitates about buying, is it right and fair to him and to myself to treat him and endeavor to demonstrate a sale, as I know that both he and I will benefit therefrom? Would this be coercion?

ANSWER—It is never right to seek in any way to coerce the mentality of any individual, but it is right to know that intelligence will guide you to the people who need that which you have to offer, and it is right to know that intelligence completes its own work and that there can be nothing in you which can obstruct or delay the perfect fulfillment of the law of right action.

TREATING FOR A POSITION

Question—Can you help me to work to obtain a certain position which I have filled before?

ANSWER—If this position is really yours, and it is right for you to have it, nothing can keep you out of it. In the divine harmony, you are a part of the Perfect Whole and cannot be out of place. Know in your innermost soul that what is yours is always yours, and that you are in your right place now, no matter what appearances may indicate. Remember, you must convince your own mind of the truth. "It is the subjective state of your thought that determines your experience." So the thing to remember is that you are now in your right place. Drop the thought of this particular position and use the larger conception in your meditation. If this *is* the place, your mental work will place you in it.

ESTABLISHING FAITH

Question—I am a firm believer in the efficacy of prayer and for many months have prayed earnestly that God would grant me a share of the great plenteousness which is everywhere, but so far I have not been able to demonstrate. A friend told me that when I ask I must believe that I have already received, but I cannot believe when I am in such straitened circumstances that I am prosperous. Will you kindly advise me as to the right thought I must hold?

ANSWER—You are blinded by what you are looking at. The sense of sight is showing you a picture that is impressing itself into your subjective mind. This picture is composed of elements which you do not wish to have manifested as objective experience.

The thing for you to do is to close your eyes to appearances and realize that before you call, you are answered. If it is hard for you to feel this truth, treat yourself for greater receptivity to your good. This will entail a total renunciation of the evidences of the senses. In your inner, secret, knowing Self, where abides the Divine Presence and Power, *you are known to be* a perfect part of the great abundant Life, and when you can believe this and learn to look upon your life as being rich and abundant, you will see the law begin to manifest for your good. In treatment, meditate on this, and speak your word as follows:

"Behind the law that obeys, upholds, executes and fulfills, there is Love. Both law and love are resident in the true Self of everyone, therefore this law and love are within me. I speak my word into this law for the cleansing of unbelief, and my subjective mind is now cleansed of all doubt and denial. I am not receptive to any element in the objective that denies my abundant life and expression, and I receive my infinite supply now. I realize that as I believe, it is done unto me; therefore I know that abundance is mine now to enjoy and experience. I am open and receptive to all my good, and I know that I receive because I now obey the law, and *believe* that I do receive."

WRITING

Question—I write good stories but they are too devoid of crime and intrigue to be in demand. Do you think I can make a success in this work?

ANSWER—There is no reason why you cannot succeed in writing stories. Sit daily and contemplate yourself as a center of this particular success. Treat the case just as you would treat for any other objective fulfillment. Realize that all of experience is a story. It is the recorded action of unseen causes. If you want an experience of success, plant your word, which is your mold in the creative substance of mind, and *know* beyond all shadow of doubting that the law will fulfill your desire.

Speak your word *feeling* the deep truth of it:

"I realize that before I call I am answered, and I know that my word is authority and law unto this activity, and the Mind in me which gives me the substance of this story knows just how to write it. I know that within that Mind is my direction and guidance, and by my word I open all channels for my success to flow in and through me. I am compelled by this inner guidance to contact the right people, to say and do whatever is necessary to help in projecting my desire on my path of experience. I am filled with success consciousness here and now, and I *know it.*"

PROBLEM OF LACK AND LIMITATION

Question—Our problem has been one of lack and limitation ever since we can remember, and we ask to be helped and guided to overcome it so that our financial conditions will improve.

ANSWER—Money is an objective representation of an eternal substance which forever flows and which is forever manifesting itself in the visible world. Drop all problems from your mind and seek to realize this substance as flowing to you and taking the definite form of every specific need. The whole endeavor is to gain a position of positive belief and acceptance. We enter the absolute in such degree as we withdraw from the relative. Our faith cannot be placed in two principles, hence let us desert the lesser and cling to the greater. Know that there is an intelligence guiding your affairs, that this intelligence is perfect and that the law of this intelligence is immutable. Know that it is flowing to you, through you and for you right now, and keep on knowing this until you make your demonstration.

WHEN PROSPERITY SEEMS WITHHELD

Question—I feel that I am not receiving that which I know is coming to me. I am unable to locate the cause why prosperity is withheld from me. I have tried to be faithful in prayer, to be positive and expectant and to know that the sources from which good can come to me are now open. I have tried not to be anxious or to worry. What shall I do?

ANSWER—Why not throw your entire mind open to the influx of prosperity, forgetting any particular channel, but rather seeking to gain such an atmosphere of abundance in your own thought that it refuses to accept the evidence of particular facts to the contrary. Do not limit the possibilities of the manifestation of the Infinite Source to one particular channel. Open wide every door and window of your mind. While this may seem rather difficult it is still possible and you will gradually come to see that the principle which you are using has resources at its command beyond your present expectation or realization.

COMMON SENSE

Question—Is planning to make one dollar cover necessities that cost two, thinking of lack?

ANSWER—It is not a thought of abundance. Whatever we do, we wish to demonstrate ahead of us; we wish to have the way prepared before us. If I had only one dollar I would spend only one dollar, but I would try to recognize the presence of that substance which is adequate supply, knowing that the Divine abundance is manifest. Troward says that God does not put money in our pocketbooks by a conjuring trick. We are the extension of It, hence intelligent plans and methods, when they present themselves to the mind, should be followed. For right action is a lengthening out of the right thought.

MEETING DULL CONDITIONS

Question—With business conditions dull in our line, my position is in jeopardy. I am doing only about half the work I formerly did and do not feel that I am earning my salary. I like to be kept busy. Will you help me with this problem?

ANSWER—To change the appearance of "dull" business conditions when the race mind is believing in inactivity calls for definite and specific mental work, but since one working consciously with the law is greater than the total race mind working unconsciously contrary to it, the change can be accomplished. Speak only the words which you wish to have returned to you as conditions. Know that for every demand there is a supply and that there is *no* obstruction to right action. Neutralize the negative pictures which are impressing themselves in subjective mind. Mentally "see" the pictures as you verbally build them. *"The word alone is conscious."* The law obeys your word. Therefore *each day* know that you are actively and rightly occupied and that the law of substance flowing through you shapes all of your affairs into patterns of success. Your prosperity is inevitable and is yours *here* and *now*.

CHANGING PROFESSIONS

Question—I am in the business world, but have been trained for and love the artistic in the realm of music and drama. How may I get back into the work that I love?

ANSWER—Treat to know that you are now in the place which will best express you, which will bring to you the greatest degree of happiness, which will the most perfectly express through you Divine Wisdom, Intelligence and Love. Place yourself in mind and in spirit in unity with your desire and stay there until it objectifies.

A PROFESSIONAL PROBLEM

Question—I am unable to attract business in my profession. I have tried consistently and earnestly to "Be still and know" that all is well. I sincerely wish to serve; I do not think first of the money. I have prayed that I may have an average of 20 patients a day. Is this unscientific? If so, how shall I work?

ANSWER—I would not treat to have any particular number of people come to me for this is a sense of limitation, but I should work to know that the continuous activity of the Spirit is manifest in my life and affairs and that those people whom I am able to help will be consciously and definitely directed to me and that there is nothing in me which can hinder my word from accomplishing.

THINKING THROUGH

Question—Owing to financial reverses, our problem is not only health and happiness for the immediate family, but inability to help our daughter finish her college course. How shall we work?

ANSWER—The prevailing condition of your affairs, physical and financial, needs to be dealt with definitely and specifically. My advice to you is to step out of the picture entirely. Get in touch with the Omnipotent Power from which all power is evolved. He who desires permanent success of any kind will find it only within—it is an unfoldment. Come in contact with the Divine Within. Power comes through repose. Be *still* and recognize the power that is at work for you *now*.

Financial success will be quickened into action by the steady and persistent recognition of success. Know that there is no obstruction to right action, and say something like this:

"I know that everything necessary to the full and complete expression of perfect adjustment in all my affairs is here and now manifesting for me, and that my word is *perfect* and harmonizes into right action everything in my life. I am success—I am physically and financially free.''

BUSINESS CHANGE

Question—If, in fact, a person's business is not prosperous, although he conscientiously, to the best of his knowledge, is endeavoring to follow the guidance of Universal Mind and Wisdom, and if indications suggest a change of location, would it be the part of wisdom to try the change of location, rather than attempt to demonstrate a prosperous business in the old location?

ANSWER—The way to demonstrate the above-named proposition is to take the mental stand that, as an idea of Truth, man is always in his right place. This "right place" includes happiness, harmony and abundance, peace, poise and power.

Prosperity is a part of the natural order of the universe. We are as successful as our vision allows us to be. We should keep the mental vision above adversity and never allow the mind to agree that any place is outside the divine order.

If, in demonstrating this, a change in location is necessary the way will be opened without confusion and we shall enter the new field without hurry or worry. *We must wait until the change is thrust upon us or until the desire to act is dominant and becomes an irresistible tendency of our thought.*

Remember that a correct treatment is both cause and effect and will open the way and compel us to walk in that way. The words spoken into being in treatment provide the way and guide our steps aright if we have confidence in them.

MEETING MONEY PROBLEMS

Question—Health, happiness, and agreeable disposition, etc., seem like real things to work for, but the only time I am really interested in mastering finance is when I need money and that is surely a poor time to be without it. I can do many things well, but am not worth a cent in finding the place in which to do them. The rent of a house is my only source of income. It has been vacant since December. I would like to sell it and also the one in which I live. I depend for money on a son's generosity—not a nice thing to do. Can you help me solve the money problem?

ANSWER—Perhaps if you would cease placing your dependence upon any person and turn your thoughts directly to the inward principle of self-perpetuating and self-manifesting existence you would remove a complex in your mind which is making it impossible for good to come to you, other than through one source. In doing mental work we resolve things into ideas and proceed upon the basis that thought will take form in the material world and that conditions are the objective outcome and physical manifestation of subjective concepts. Try to sense yourself as being surrounded by plenty, and do not look to any particular source for the manifestation of this abundance.

OUTLINING THE CHANNEL

Question—What do you mean by not outlining or indicating the channel through which good must come?

ANSWER—Not indicating the channel means that we must not look to one certain place for our good, expecting that it must come from that source only. We must be definite and specific in asking for the manifestation we desire, but we must leave the way of its manifestation to that Mind that knows just how to bring it about. For instance: We will say we want sunshine in the room. If the room is full of windows and we know of the presence of only one window, we will naturally look to that one only as the avenue through which the sunlight can enter. Consequently the beam of light we receive will be many times smaller than if we recognized that light could come through all the windows. Mentally seeing only one channel limits the working out to one place or way of manifestation, whereas if you know all channels are open and trust the way of manifestation to God, to All Good, you have left a free field in which all the agencies necessary to fulfillment may act.

Man's business is to set the law in motion. God's business is to outline. Open the door and have an unfailing faith that "Only my good can come to me, and that underneath are the everlasting arms."

IN TIME OF DESPAIR

Question—My husband passed on some months ago and I am faced with earning my living and I don't seem to be able to do it. Please advise me.

ANSWER—The aftermath of the passing of one's companion is often fraught with what appears to be insurmountable obstacles. Frequently, radical and fundamental changes have to be made in one's new adjustment to life and experience. There is great danger of becoming negative at such a time and, through the unconscious practice of a negative state of mind, attracting undesirable conditions into one's experience.

The treatment for you is to know there is that within you which knows the solution to your problem, and It hears and responds when you call. Become so sure of this that you will turn automatically to this Indwelling Comforter for the fulfillment of every need you have.

If you have honestly done *everything* you can toward obtaining employment, try to realize that no seeking is vain. If there are no apparent results at present, get the truth firmly established in your mind that your seeking is part of a divine promise. "Ye shall find" because you have diligently sought. You have opened avenues and made contacts that will benefit you.

In treating, follow this method:

Sitting quietly, clear your mind of every earthly need and try to feel the truth about yourself—you are *whatever* God is, in essence, substance, and power. Whatever It is that upholds and sustains the order and rhythm of the limitless Cosmos, is also the heart and core of your life. Once you realize this, no experience can rob you of the positive assurance that *all is well with you.*

Say: "In this great One Mind, there is perfect order, perfect activity, perfect harmony and perfect ease. I, being a part of this Allness, am in my right place now, in my right activity now. I know with the Mind of God within me that my problem is already solved and that the solution presents itself in my conscious mind for my guidance. I trust this guidance and obey it willingly, and it leads me to my right employment. I thank God for my living faith and trust in the unfailingness of His Love through immutable law in my life and affairs."

Do not despair. *Work* at this on the plane of the Absolute, or Cause, and the relative, or visible effect, will manifest for you. Believe with all your soul that your problem is *now* solved, to your entire satisfaction. All the work in the world is ineffective without faith.

DEBT

Question—I would like to know what thoughts are useful for the collection of debts?

ANSWER—What is yours must come to you. That is law. The first definite thing to do is to put out of your consciousness all ideas that someone owes you. If you would have no debt, see mentally no one owing you and see yourself at peace with everyone concerned. Spirit never fails us. Dissolve belief in duality and misunderstanding, and know there is nothing but right and harmonious action. We are not dealing with the person or condition, but we deal always with mind and plunge beneath the surface of things and neutralize the false condition by the spoken word. Treat as follows: "By my word which is Pure Spirit I wipe out of mind *all* debt. All that the Father has *is* mine and there is no person, thing or condition to deny me what is rightfully mine. I claim my own *now* in peace and harmony. Every avenue and door is open for my good; every agency necessary to the fulfillment of my word *now* serves me to this end."

MAKING A CHANGE

Question—I am puzzled how to start in the practice of Religious Science. I want to leave my present position for another with more future. Can you help me?

ANSWER—In the practice of Religious Science relative to the particular situation, you would not leave your present position until a better were offered. You should work to know that that Divine Intelligence within you, which is already one with all good, is now establishing you in that place which is best suited to your abilities. Then you should wait for the outcome of this treatment, which will certainly produce the desired result. In this way there need be no anxiety nor strain, but rather a calm sense of peace and certainty and a willingness to let the law operate.

EXPLANATION OF HYPNOTIC BELIEFS

Question—I am an amateur practitioner, working for a friend who, I fear, neutralizes my efforts on his behalf. What should I do?

ANSWER—Your belief that he can neutralize your work gives his negative thought the very power you should deny. You are seeing two powers; one for and one against the desired result. It matters not what he says or does; you are not working with his thought. You are working with your own, and with yourself, alone. You must heal yourself—your own mind. Your work begins and ends within your own mind. Clear your own thought. Know that the word you speak is the law for him. Know that there is nothing to oppose your word because your word for him is the Word of God for him—and in this Word there can be only right action. Cease to see any importance in anything that throws doubt or confusion into your own thought-stream.

DETAILS IN TREATMENT

Question—Can spiritual treatment be given successfully for prosperity without knowledge by the practitioner of the details of the patient's business affairs?

ANSWER—It is not necessary for the practitioner to know every detail of a person's affairs in order to help him. Yet very frequently when the practitioner does know of the operation of the thought of the one he is seeking to help, he is able to analyze the condition and point to the wrong conception. However, we should not worry about this but should realize that since the lesser is contained in the greater, the more complete consciousness we have of good, the more specific good we shall experience.

THAT WHICH IS YOURS

Question—My employer is a contractor and I believe thoroughly honest. Although I have sold a number of properties for him, for some unknown reason he thus far has not offered to pay me for my work. How shall I treat in his case?

ANSWER—Your treatment to bring that which is yours to you should be along the following lines:

In your daily meditation, enter into that quiet place within your own mind where you realize that justice rules and that your good cannot be kept from you; that the unchangeable Principle, perfect and complete, knows your need and fulfills it. Then speak your word as follows:

"I know that Indwelling Intelligence within me knows the ways and means by which all my affairs are adjusted in the right way now. My word opens avenues and channels for my success, and I claim now that which is mine; there is no counter claim in my law of good. I am grateful to my indwelling Christ for *all my good* and I feel certain that my expectancy shall be and is fulfilled."

FEAR OF TAKING INITIATIVE

Question—How can I overcome an inferiority complex, resulting in fear—fear of taking initiative?

ANSWER—An inferiority complex can exist only in an erroneous conception of oneself. If man could realize that there is nothing but the One Perfect Life, whose Perfect Intelligence knows all diversity of form as perfect parts of Itself, the idea of superiority or inferiority would dissolve in this conviction. The real Self of man is pure Spirit. This Spirit knows no comparisons. It knows only perfection. Man, in the visible world, created the idea of comparison; thus, we have large, larger, largest; small, smaller, smallest, etc. The truth is that each thing is perfect.

An inferiority complex has its foundation in the oldest enemy—fear. Fear of criticism stops initiative. "He who never made a mistake never made anything." Fear of criticism is a form of egotism, and can be indulged until it results in a physical disease. Jumpy nerves always accompany acute fears. The fear-suggestion becomes so habitual that it fills the most harmless and commonplace action with dread. There is no slavery so cruel as the slavery of one's fears.

Since you realize that fear is at the bottom of your trouble, the first step is for you to look the fact squarely in the face. Realize that fear inhibits all right action, dams the flow of life, steals a man's birthright of freedom of thought and action. The next step is to determine to be rid of it. Vision yourself gathering up your fears, one by one, naming each one, piling them in a heap, and setting fire to them, as you would burn rubbish. These fears were but false faces that had covered the truth from your mental sight. Now that they have been destroyed, treat yourself for poise and assurance. Say, "I have destroyed every false and damming influence in my subjective mind and I declare myself free forever. I know myself to be filled with the initiative of the Spirit, which directs my thought and action and compels me to do the right thing at the right time. I cooperate willingly with this Inner Guidance and obey it without hesitation. I realize myself to be a perfect part of the Perfect Whole, and in this consciousness there can be no false suggestion of inferiority or fear of any kind."

Then be firm with yourself. Declare the truth about yourself and feel safe in the words you utter, for your words "are Life and they are Truth."

REMOVING STUMBLING BLOCKS

Question—If one is not consciously aware of the cause of his unhappiness and lack of success, how may he speak "definitely" for the healing of a condition?

ANSWER—The first thing is to realize that you cannot speak at all without using Divine Mind, because Divine Mind is all there is. Within this Mind is the condition you wish to evolve, and this Mind knows just how to go about the evolution. It is fair to suppose that every individual would eliminate his stumbling blocks if he knew definitely what they were. Realize that the Knower within you knows all that is necessary for the manifestation of your desire, and plant your seed in this conviction.

Treatment should follow this method:

"I realize that my life is rich in love and happiness and

success, and they are now manifest in my experience. I give this desire to the Creative Substance and the Law, in the full knowledge that the God within me knows how the manifestation shall objectify, and that He surely brings it forth for my enjoyment. I accept it now, for it is finished."

After you have accepted it, it is yours.

COLLECTING AN UNCERTAIN DEBT

Question—I helped a young man to start in business. He has paid me from time to time, but more than half of the debt is still due. We did not draw up any legal papers, so he is morally but not legally bound to repay me. I am filled with criticism and anxiety. Please advise me how to think this proposition through.

ANSWER—Begin your work definitely and scientifically and do not look to the person or to conditions as your means of supply. As you free yourself in your own mind from the possession of this particular money, you will free the young man also, and if you speak the right constructive word, your money will come to you. *As one door closes, another opens.* The treatment should be after this fashion: "I know that the Spirit of Infinite Goodness is operating in and through me, around me and for me, and I know that this Spirit of Infinite Goodness is the Spirit of Limitless Power, and is governed by immutable law. There is no loss, and my own cannot be kept from me. I know that everything I should have is brought to me without struggle or strain. I now claim from the Universal my abundant supply. That which I have given, I bless, knowing it must return to me blessed, and I know that whatever agencies are necessary for the fulfillment of my word are actively working for me now. The power of this word is *instant,* since the Word is Pure Spirit. I expect and receive my good now."

A BUSINESS PROBLEM

Question—How can I solve this problem: For $5000 I purchased the interest and goodwill of my associate in business, on condition that he should not engage in the same business within one year. He violated this agreement and now has opened a place of business near me and has hired one of my best employees.

ANSWER—In the working out of your problem it is necessary to resolutely put out of your mind any thought of competition or any belief that anything can be taken away from you. Since you are dealing with the absolute truth, it cannot know loss and has no competitor. Do not waste any time wondering what other people are doing, or worrying over the non-fulfillment of their contracts, but be sure that your own contract with the principle which you are seeking to demonstrate never becomes violated. This contract which you have made with the principle of your being is one wherein you have promised continuously to believe that there is an invisible and intelligent power daily guiding and sustaining your efforts, an All-knowing Mind motivating your purposes. Never count the strength of the enemy but look into the One and your demonstration will be made.

THE IDEA OF SACRIFICE

Question—Is it possible to heal one who is of the old faith— who apparently believes everything is possible with God, but that He sends illness and that patient suffering teaches a great lesson?

ANSWER—Why should one who believes that God sends illness desire to be healed? It would seem that, if this belief were sincere, the sufferer would gladly undergo whatever discomfort God sent for so great a cause!

When the patient is convinced that only health can flow

from the fountain springs of Life, of God, he can be healed. But it will be necessary to point out to such a person the love of God and all His goodness, which needs the suffering of no one to augment it. He must be shown that the well man is the glory of God because he manifests the health of God; that the happy, harmonious, prosperous man is the God-man, because he evinces these God-attributes of well-being. The idea of sacrifice must be lost entirely. God, in His completeness, needs and desires the sacrifice of no one thing or person or condition in order to gain another. In the measureless depth of His substance of all good, such a thing as sacrifice is unnecessary. Convince your patient that God is within *him*, in all His completeness, as Life Itself, enacting all the laws of His creative Selfhood, and it is possible to so enlighten him that a healing will be the result.

REMOVING OBSTRUCTION

Question—Teaching is my profession. I completed my university course last June, and while I have all the requirements necessary to fill a teaching position, my lack of experience in such work has so far been a great drawback to me in my search for employment. I would like to know just how to work against this apparent obstruction, "inexperience," which has faced me wherever I have applied.

ANSWER—Obstruction is obstruction, no matter by what name it is called. If yours has been called "inexperience," it should be treated just as any other stumbling block would be. If you can believe that you can sidestep this hindrance, the way will open for you to do so. Recognize that the inner Wisdom which contemplates you from the center of your being sees no obstruction in your path. It is from this center that all evolution emerges. Quoting from *The Science of Mind*, "Every thought sets the Law in motion, specializing It for some definite purpose; in this way the word becomes the law unto the thing spoken." So if you would be free forever from that word "inexperience," first drop it from your own contemplation as a power, and set about getting ready for your demonstration. Daily sit in meditation. This is vitally important. Once or twice is not enough. Persevere until your word returns to you bearing the fruits of its seed. Realize in meditation that you are equipped for the certain, definite work of teaching, that you want a teaching position, that there is such a position for you now in Divine Mind, and that you are established in it. This specializes the Law, and all its action is focused on producing the position you have deposited in Mind. Thank God that you have received your position, and believe this is true with all your heart. All outlining is left to Mind, which knows how to execute the pattern you give it and sets whatever agencies that are necessary to work to that end. Know in your conscious mind that "inexperience" is a false power and that it has no claim on you, and cannot stand in the presence of your spoken word. Be not discouraged if you meet it again and again. You have obliterated it by denying it power, and it must fade from the picture to trouble you no more. For your word is God in action, and since God is for you, who can be against you?

USING METAPHYSICS IN SCHOOL WORK

Question—Having trouble with one subject at the University, I devote a great deal of time to preparation of my assignments, yet examinations show low grades. I am not working solely for high grades, yet they are indications of the amount of work understood. What can I do?

ANSWER—Very likely you have the idea that this subject is beyond your understanding and you are seeing it as difficult. Ideas work themselves out into conditions, as you know. Therefore, the thing for you to do is to cease believing that any subject is beyond your understanding. Know that *That* which is doing the knowing within your consciousness cannot be other than true to Its own nature. *And that nature is to know.* Therefore, keep all sense of burden out of your work and ask the Divine Intelligence within to reveal to your consciousness the perfect understanding of the subject before you. "Seek and ye *shall find.*" Say in treatment:

"The Mind in me and the Mind within the subject are One; therefore, I do know. And this Knowing presses *now* into my consciousness and I am aware of the meaning of this subject."

DECISION WHERE OTHERS ARE INVOLVED

Question—I find myself in an almost unbearable situation. In any decision I may make, others are involved, therefore I hesitate to make a move. Am I right in staying on, being patient and knowing things will work out all right, or am I just weak?

ANSWER—"He who hesitates is lost." If you know that a decision is necessary, and that it will eventually clear the atmosphere for you and for all concerned, make it and get it over with. Vacillating can develop into a negative habit. Knowing that things will work out satisfactorily in the long run is all right if it makes for the general harmony of everyone, and if it is not merely postponing to a future indefinite date a mental task that is distasteful now, but sooner or later must be done. To shun responsibility is weakness. Your very weakness has become such a burden to you that you find yourself in an "unbearable situation." Speak your mind. And stand by your word. Keep your own equanimity—if others lose theirs. Decide what your action shall be in the case and always with love in your heart for all, stand by your decision. God works through positive characters, courageous characters.

Know that you will be right in your course of action, because you are guided by that Indwelling Wisdom that knows and answers every call you make on It.

ACCEPTING TEMPORARY POSITION

Question—When mental work is being done for securing a position of a certain kind in accordance with one's abilities and experience and a minor position is offered, should one accept it?

ANSWER—When one is working out problems as suggested by this question, he should be willing to follow his demonstration step by step, knowing that each step is a movement in the right direction. Thus he rejects nothing and accepts everything. Since we do not see the principle at work we cannot always understand the reason for certain steps being taken. But with the right mental vision behind our work and the right objective method on our part we are led, sometimes gradually but always certainly, to the desired goal.

GETTING NEW START

Question—A few years ago we lost a great deal of money. Since then it has been hard to get a good start. Now we have become interested in a business which looks good but we need some help to overcome fear. Please tell us how to proceed to feel assured of prosperity and right action in this business.

ANSWER—I should work to know that the Spirit of Truth within me, which is God and which is perfect intelligence as well as right action, is directing every move and compelling right action in every instance in my life. Work to remove not only the sense of doubt but also the sense of loss. The mind should come to feel that there has been no real loss, since the Spirit of wholeness can never lose anything. The endeavor in spiritual treatment is to bring to the mind a realization that this Spirit of wholeness is our own active spirit right now, producing right results in everything we do. Shift the burden of any sense of load or any personal responsibility over into an assuming that the law is both willing and able to direct your actions and bring affairs into perfect harmony with itself.

CONFRONTED BY LACK

Question—How can I keep from thinking lack and limitation when I am confronted by it many, many times a day?

Answer—We can demonstrate to the level of our ability to know; beyond this we cannot go. . . . The student should take time every day to see his life as he wishes it to be, to make a mental picture of his ideal. He should pass this picture over to the Law and go about his business with the inner assurance that on the invisible side of life something is taking place. Let the Law work through and express Itself in the experience.

You cannot see tomorrow, nor next summer. But they will come because it is their nature to appear according to their law. You can picture the roses that will grow in your garden next summer, because you *know* the plants are there. Just so, plant your thought for the experience you desire, *knowing* that on the unseen side of life, "something is taking place." If you can train yourself to *know* what you cannot see with your eyes, your knowing will project what you desire into visibility and experience.

TO BETTER ONE'S POSITION

Question—My husband has an intermittent job. He must have steady work with a regular salary. Please tell us how to think?

Answer—The first and fundamental principle of continuous prosperity is to realize definitely and positively that those things and conditions which you desire are possible. Through your spoken word you can realize all that belongs to you by divine right. Putting out of your thought the apparent fluctuation which marks periods of employment and unemployment, take your stand for the condition you desire to have manifested. Work to know that your word spoken into Mind returns to you quickly bearing its perfect fruit. Know that through right avenues and right channels, the right opportunities for steady employment come to him (your husband); that there is *no* obstruction between him and his perfect employment; that he is divinely active and occupied fully, and abundantly remunerated for his work. Know definitely that he gratefully accepts every opportunity that presents itself for his highest good. Know that Subjective Mind accepts the idea, and your supply will manifest in your life.

VISUALIZING A SUM OF MONEY

Question—I am on a small salary with a large family. In demonstrating more money, must I visualize a certain amount, or should I see myself as supplied with money at all times?

ANSWER—In working for more money, realize first the infinity of substance, formed and unformed, which is pressing upon you from every direction. Realize that this substance waits for your mold—your word; that it shapes itself according to the content of your word; that your word is pure Spirit, declaring itself into the form you desire. In this realization, speak out your desire somewhat as follows: "I know that this word which I speak now returns to me in the form of the fulfilled thing which I desire, and I know that all the positive forces of the universe wait upon my word and serve it. Only my good can come to me, and that which is for my highest good cannot be withheld from me."

Stimulate your consciousness with rich and constructive and Godlike ideas. If you do, you may be sure that the Law will act and will become powerfully operative to that end. Visualize abundance, and see every channel and avenue open for your good.

OVERCOMING LACK OF CONFIDENCE

Question—I should like some help to do a little straight thinking, as I am taking up a new line of work which requires more self-assurance than I seem to possess. I feel that I lack confidence in my own ability, yet I have the knowledge and experience necessary to make a success of this venture.

ANSWER—Fear or concern about ability to undertake something new presupposes duality. In reality all work (everything) is contained within the infinitude of the great whole. Nothing is new, nothing is unknown to Infinite Mind. To admit a doubt of one's ability is a misconception of that which is. Eliminate the idea of separateness, and endeavor to unify your consciousness with the thought that there is no limitation in Infinite Intelligence.

Treat believing that: "Infinite Intelligence within me knows itself to be the Creator of all situations. It knows that there is *nothing* with which it cannot cope, and it succeeds in doing, through me, everything required in my new line of work. My intelligence is this Infinite Intelligence in operation."

STARTING A NEW WORK

Question—I am starting a new work very soon which I believe to be my big opportunity, and I wish to be a perfect channel through which Divine Mind can operate successfully. Will you help me?

ANSWER—You have begun your new enterprise in a very constructive frame of mind, so there is every reason to believe you will be successful. Your willingness to be an unobstructed channel, if persisted in, must terminate satisfactorily.

In your meditation realize that Good governs all your affairs, that It makes the right contacts and compels you to think, say and do the right thing at the right time. Know that this Good Governor is all the activity there is in your world, and that It has your personal interests in Its wise and sure keeping.

Each day bless your place of business and name it a point of Success for yourself, a point where the presence of your good manifests. Never doubt, no matter what appearances may declare. See through them to the ideal, and "stay at home with Cause." The effect will take care of itself.

NOTHING IS EVER LOST

Question—I have lost my home. The mortgage company has gathered in what it has taken me a lifetime to establish. How can I reconcile this fact with your teaching that nothing is ever lost?

ANSWER—Changes come. However hard it may be for us to accept them, we are compelled to meet them. Our reaction is most important; it is by our reactions to circumstances that we measure our weakness or strength. The entire emotional field of our being is affected by our reactions to experiences. You say your home is lost that you have been a "lifetime establishing." We cannot see behind the scenes and check all the whys and wherefores for your losing it. But we can say to you: Stand fast. Know that if you could establish one "home" you can establish another. Yes, I know we hear contrary opinions all about us. But consider this: Is the possession of a house and lot really a home? Is not the state of mind much more of a home than the physical place you have known as a number on a certain street? The very spirit which built that ideal home is the Everlasting Spirit which builds the universe all about us. The law of "home" is everywhere.

ESTABLISHING BUSINESS HARMONY

Question—If harmony is not established, we will lose our business. One partner is trying to freeze out the other and a big company is waiting to take over the concession if the drilling is not done. How can we meet this situation by mental realization?

ANSWER—It is very essential in your case to establish harmony in your own consciousness relating to your partner. The thing to do is to look through this situation and refuse to accept obstruction in any form, but steadily declare for right action. The fundamental error which brought about this condition is a belief in duality—a lack of realization of the unity of life. Recognize but the One Mind. See God in each one connected with this property, and the trouble will be healed. Do not waste your divine forces in condemnation. Keep your thought-stream clear and your central idea firmly placed in God, the All Good. In your treatment know definitely that, "My harmony is built upon Principle and it is unfailing. The law of harmony is the law of my life and I know it is mine now, perfect and complete. And I know that harmony expresses itself into everything that I do, say or think. And I know there is no Presence other than the Perfect Mind, and in this Mind and Spirit I am free, happy, abundantly provided for, and everything in the Universe knows I am established in the Center of harmony." Be unafraid and know that, "only my good can come to me."

PART V

Miscellaneous Questions and Answers

THE OLD HABIT TRACK

Question—Why is it that when some persons start to study metaphysics everything seems to go wrong for a while?

ANSWER—A beginner in metaphysics is reversing his thought processes. He is running back over the old habit track and encountering all those forms he would eliminate. He must blaze new thought trails, make new pictures of which he is the acting center or magnet. If he has formerly been vindictive, wrongly aggressive, selfish and arbitrary, these traits of character will rise before him continuously seeking the old recognition and indulgence. If he is off guard for a time, he will find them obtruding themselves at most inconvenient and embarrassing moments. If he does not understand how they happen to come into his consciousness, he will fight them with his will and thus be on the wrong track. But if he realizes they are old pictures of his own creating, he may bid them depart and turn his attention to the conditions he wishes to see manifested.

The beginner in metaphysics is deliberately choosing a higher vibration, or state of consciousness, and to attain it consciously, he has to clear out all the strangling, obstructing undergrowth of the old subjective field. Herein he proves that he has no fight—that his choice and his word have set the law into greater activity and he is automatically lifted to the plane of his desire.

IMMORTALITY EXPLAINED

Question—Where does the resurrection life begin and what takes place?

ANSWER—There is no resurrection life as opposed to another life. There is no immortality as opposed to mortality, any more than there is a Divine Mind which is opposed to the human. The universe refuses to be divided. Jesus understood this when he said, "God is not a God of the dead but of the living for all live unto Him." Life does not know death nor can it produce it. If it could it would be self-destructive.

UNIFY WITH FELLOWMEN

Question—I am alone in the world and must work for my living. When I get a position I try my best, but sooner or later I am let out—never on account of inefficiency, but because I will not stoop to deceit, running to the manager with gossip or not caring for the conversation of the others. Can you help me to overcome this condition?

ANSWER—Man has been called the "social animal." By this is meant that he must meet advances from and make advances to his fellowman. "No man liveth to himself alone," the scriptures tell us. If you are habitually unsocial, inclined to be a bit self-righteous, you will find yourself to be a misfit wherever you are.

Cease declaring yourself to be alone. Realize the One is Everpresent, Omnipotent and willing to befriend you. The only way Universal Love can help a person is *through* the person. If you will permit love to flow through you toward your fellowmen, you will find them seeking you out. They will befriend you in a thousand ways, but *you* must open the door. *You* must be receptive and friendly. *You* must *let* people know that you really *like* them. Adopt a friendly attitude toward everything and everybody. See the good in people and ignore such qualities as do not please you. Stop resisting others. A *persistent* effort to expand your appreciation of the good in others, of their desirability as friends, will inevitably open avenues through which your social and business success may flow to you.

Declare in the treatment that there is no misunderstanding, no resistance, no deceit in Divine Mind. Destroy the belief in inequality—recognize that there is but One Mind. See God in *all* and the trouble will soon be healed. Come into the realization of the full unity of all life and you will find that only happy solutions will obtain in your business and social contacts.

DEVELOPING POWER OF DECISION

Question—For years I have cared for my mother. She was a very forceful character, dominating my entire life . . . not with a conscious desire to do so, but simply by the habit of years and a thought that she was caring for me. She has recently died and I find myself like a ship without a rudder, having no initiative or power of decision. I realize now what has happened to me. Is it too late to develop some will power?

ANSWER—Far from being too late to develop the latent power within, it is the ideal time for your expression, not only for such development, but for the reshaping of your whole reaction to experience. You *must* now take charge of your own affairs, using your own creative power. For a while it may be difficult for you to break old habits and assert yourself in your mental world, but do not be discouraged. Know that you were intended to do your own thinking; proceed to do so at once and work diligently at your conscious development. None of your divine inheritance has been lost through your non-use of individual thought; it is all there at your call, but you must learn that it has to reach you through new paths in mind.

By faithfully sitting in daily meditation, consciously accepting your power to decree and to decide, you build another habit that will make you positive by dethroning the old power that has so long coerced you. Assert yourself now and claim your birthright of freedom in perfect love before another dominant "mind" appears in your experience. This moment is yours for development, self-assertion, and for freeing yourself from that slave consciousness.

In your meditation say: "Loving Giver of all my good, I thank You for my blessed freedom from mental slavery. I know that You give me power to think for myself, *now*— that You guide me in all my actions now; that You protect me from mistakes. I know that Divine Intelligence within me guides and directs me, and this faith and assurance I have, that all the good in the universe inspires me to think, say and do only the right thing."

GUIDANCE FOR CHILD

Question—How, in a child of eight, would you erase the idea that everything is hard work?

ANSWER—In working for your child realize that he is a perfect idea in Infinite Mind, that there are no hard places or difficult situations in Mind, that behind everything there is only the *One,* and that he—the child—exists at the standpoint of opportunity for self-expression. Take the time each day to know for him that everything right here and now is made known to him without effort or struggle and he is free; that the intelligence within him directs and guides him, and the perfect law governs him at all times.

AN APPRECIATION OF FUN

Question—I meet people socially who have the ability to converse in an interesting manner. Their words are of very light character—but everybody is happy. I have nothing to say and feel awkward and out of place when in this really charming company. How may I learn to enjoy their conversation and reply in like vein?

ANSWER—A well-rounded mental development includes an appreciation of fun, and it is as natural for intellectuals to play as it is for children and kittens. Know deep within yourself that you are not different from your friends. Seek them often and force yourself to play with them, to talk with them, to really *meet* them mentally. It may seem absurd at first, but if you can remember that you are actually reestablishing your mental equilibrium by so doing, you will realize that the effort is worthwhile.

Meditate on the fact that there is but One Mind in all Life —and in It are all the faculties you will ever need. Through your thought, you direct mind-energy to the condition you desire. In your case, it is an appreciation of and ability to play. It will soon become easy, and by and by, automatic adjustment will carry you into the expression necessary for the moment.

DEVELOPING A POSITIVE ATTITUDE

Question—What would be the treatment for inertia and an indifferent attitude toward life?

ANSWER—Jesus said: "I am come that they might have life, and have it more abundantly." It would appear that his whole message to the human family was to quicken into a higher vibration the appreciation of the fact that life is present in its entirety at every point where the mind contacts it in consciousness. He knew so much more than he could teach, not because of any inability on his part, but because his followers could not comprehend what he was talking about.

A person who is indifferent toward life should "snap out" of his lethargy and stimulate his thinking with constructive reactions to life, directing the mind toward a definite purpose. Treatment would follow somewhat this plan of attack:

"I am unified with all life and all people and I give up all idea of dullness, listlessness and now I enjoy living. My life is full, complete and perfect. I love people and I realize that their activities are also mine by reflection, since we are all united in the One Life."

Now cooperate with your own words by *getting busy* along some definite line. Observe greatly and act accordingly.

OVERCOMING IRRITATION

Question—People not only irritate me but I much prefer to be alone. A condition over which I worry lately is that I do not trust my fellow beings. It used to be simply a desire to be left alone. Now it is an actual fear of what this one might say or that one might do. How can I overcome this?

ANSWER—Know that there is nothing in people which can irritate you and nothing in you which can irritate people. Try to gain a broad-gauged, tolerant attitude toward life. After all, no one has yet completely attained perfection and we are all children in Truth, all travelers on the road. We all make mistakes and most of these mistakes should be overlooked. Someday we shall learn not to be confused; we shall see through the outward differences to the inner unity of all life. In this way we join forces with the best that is in people and thereby bring the good to the surface. Try this for a while and see what effect it will have.

A MOTHER'S PROBLEM

Question—How can I overcome sorrow and loneliness caused by separation and not hearing from my two daughters?

ANSWER—"Love fulfilleth the Law." If you will realize perfect freedom for your daughters, you will be working the law for your own freedom. "Loose them" and know that there is no separation in mind. The very mind current that flows through your own consciousness flows through that of your daughters. Be very sure that you leave them in peace and freedom to write you or not, as they choose. Your work has to do with yourself alone, and as soon as you feel confident that your word is really true, your letters from them will be forthcoming. Do not merely hope. *Know it.* In your meditation to dispel this condition, treat something like this: "I know that there is no separation, no misunderstanding, no inharmony in Divine Mind; and I know that Love fulfills Itself in my desire and that there is nothing between me and (naming them) that has the power to keep us apart. In love I know them to be divinely free and I give them the freedom that I claim for myself. I know that the love of God is flowing through them and through me, and it works out this word of mutual interest and harmonizes into right action everything in our lives. My word is law unto this thing and cannot return to me void."

BRINGING ABOUT RECONCILIATION

Question—How can I treat my son and his wife for a reconciliation of love and understanding?

ANSWER—In treating for harmony between two individuals, the persons most concerned should be held in the consciousness that they are perfect parts of the Perfect Whole, and that nothing but Perfection can touch their lives and actions. Care should be taken by the one doing the treating to give the individual perfect freedom. There should be no effort to coerce the one or the other, or to bend him or her to your own idea of harmony. Treat something like this:

"There is but One Mind, One Life, and in that One Mind and One Life there is no inharmony at any point, at any time. Since this Mind is individualized in (name son) and (name wife), there can be no inharmony in them."

A TOTAL FAILURE

Question—If there is a life hereafter, what is there to be looked forward to if this life has seemed a total failure?

ANSWER—For a man to feel that his life is a failure is to feel himself apart from God. Whether he knows it or not, man is in a law which evolves him to higher planes. Even the lowest and most hopeless savage will some time attain to Christ consciousness.

Life *is* God. Ignorance of this truth does not make Life a failure. The man going through the experience may be a failure in his own estimation and in that of his neighbors, but Life is unscathed. God does no futile thing, creates no lost motion. Everything has its purpose. The great mistake lies in man's looking outside himself for his future. He is his own future. His experiences are radiations of himself, set in motion by his thinking.

If the best a man can do through his earth experience is to embody the idea that Life is a failure, this will *appear* to be true to him. However, the appearance but covers the truth, that Life is God, indwelling the very soul of man. There is nothing to fear about the future. "Look well to today." An open mind, a willingness to learn from Within, a faith that God is good and that He is the essence and substance of our lives forever . . . these are enough for any man to realize that Life could not fail.

MOTHER WORRIES OVER SON

Question—My boy of 18 is so restless. He stays with me a few months and then goes away without telling me where he is going. When he is in Texas he is with friends much older than himself and they are so wild. I want him to go to school but he is so hard-headed and easily influenced by these boys, and I am almost beside myself with worry. I am only 34 and I need help so badly with this grown boy. Please tell me what to do.

ANSWER—Your problem is one of realizing that your son is an individual and must work out the evolution of his own soul. Every individual is a unique incarnation of the universal Spirit. Each has the same ultimate destiny but all do not choose the same road. Instead of trying to coerce the will and attention of your son, seek rather to realize that the Spirit within him is the directing force of his own life. Try to feel that he is being guided by an intelligent and perfect Mind. Insofar as possible, relieve your own thought of personal responsibility and obligation in the matter and you will have done two things: you will have relieved his mind of the suggestion of fear in your own thought and also you will have opened up a channel of receptivity in his thought for the influx of intelligent and constructive guidance.

SUBCONSCIOUS COMMUNICATION

Question—Is it possible for the subconscious mind of one person to communicate with the subconscious mind of another?

ANSWER—It is possible for the subconscious mind of one person to communicate with that of another. In all probability there is a continuous subjective conversation going on between those who are sympathetically inclined toward each other, and unquestionably the subjective reactions of the race consciousness constitute what psychology calls the collective unconscious, what we call the race mind, and what the Bible calls the carnal mind, which exerts a very great influence over all people. The fact of subjective communication is easily proven by the simple experiment of sitting with someone who is grief-stricken and receiving the subjective atmosphere of his thought.

COMMUNION OF SOULS

Question—You know that old saying, "Daytime is nighttime of the soul; nighttime is daytime of the soul." Is there a communion of souls aside from personal contact? Instead of contacting another in person, may one send his thought? Is not this the "Comforter" of which we read in connection with the statement, "I will not leave thee utterly alone?"

ANSWER—I do not believe that the daytime is the nighttime of the soul. That part of us which is spiritual must be the part of us which is conscious. That part of us which is subjective is the mechanical result of the spiritual and spontaneous consciousness, plus the instinctive urge which comes with us. There would be no real individuality or personality without self-conscious contacts. Hence, it seems improbable that the activities of the mind in its unconscious state could be as real as its activities while in a conscious state. While it is probable that the mind continues to work even during sleep, in this work it undoubtedly follows the suggestions and impulses which have come to it during its waking state. And in all probability there is more or less of a subjective communication going on at *all* times between persons who are in deep sympathy with one another. This communication might or might not rise to the threshold of consciousness. When it rises to the threshold of consciousness it is as a direct message or a telepathic communication. When it does not rise to the threshold of consciousness, it is more like an impulse or an urge. The "Comforter" is "Emanuel, or God with us," and a Spirit within our own mind which forever bears witness to the direct relationship between the Infinite and the finite.

PROBLEM OF ABNORMAL APPETITE

Question—Will you please help me to overcome an abnormal craving appetite for food?

ANSWER—We need to be well balanced on all three planes —spiritual, mental and physical—and it is contrary to the law of God to violate any one of God's laws. Cultivate a hobby. Become vitally interested in some line of study. Stimulate the mind with something constructive and try to realize that you do not live to *eat* and that enough food is as good as a feast. Habit will reassert itself as long as you indulge it and even for a time after you have repeatedly denied it, but the appetite will gradually become normal in its demand.

OVERCOMING SENSITIVENESS

Question—I do not think that I am as sensitive as I used to be, as I can laugh at myself and really enjoy it. But my husband! While I am learning to laugh, he is hurt at mere trifles which were never intended to hurt. Two sensitive people always together is too much. Can you help both of us to overcome this sensitiveness?

ANSWER—If both you and your husband would start with knowing that neither one wishes to offend or hurt the other, and that neither one can possibly be offended, and begin to idealize each other a little, and stop *expecting* to be sensitive or to be hurt, and be just downright good pals, with complete frankness toward each other, I think your troubles would soon be over.

THE MEANING OF PSYCHIC

Question—What do people mean when they speak of a person as being psychic?

ANSWER—From the sense of this question, a psychic would be one who is able to objectify, or bring to the threshold of the conscious mind, subjective thought-pictures and atmospheres. Since all people have a subjective life, all people are unconsciously psychic, but we ordinarily speak of one as being psychic who is able to bring these psychic pictures to the threshold of the objective consciousness. To be able to do this consciously is normal, but to do this through any other practice is abnormal. The conscious mind, intellect, and the faculty of reason should control all subjective states.

TALKING OF HEALING

Question—A friend has talked to me, asking me to give up what he calls foolishness, as he calls my faith in spiritual healing. Then he said that when people come to my home I should not mention these things to them. Is he correct?

ANSWER—If your faith in spiritual healing is sufficient, it will prove itself and there will be nothing to argue about. If your faith is not sufficient then there is nothing to be gained in arguing over it. It seems advisable not to argue but to keep on doing your mental work until you have proven your position. In this way no subjective interference is possible. Work away in your own mind. There is a power in you which will respond to your faith in it, disregarding the opinions of anyone or everyone to the contrary. But I would be very careful to refrain from all objective arguments. Keep your own thought clear, hold your own counsel within yourself and there will come to you not only an absolute assurance but a complete vindication of your inner faith.

CAN WRITER BE METAPHYSICAL?

Question—I enjoy your magazine immensely each month and would like to ask you some questions: (1) How may one use the power to accelerate a delayed musical education? (2) The metaphysical attitude is not, do you think, beneficial to a writer of fiction—who must live (mentally, at least) the conflicts of his stories?

ANSWER—All talent is subjective. It is the law of subjectivity to objectify itself. Somewhere in you there is a direct access to the Father of all characterizations and as Longfellow says, in *Hiawatha*, "to the master of all music." I see no reason why a writer or musician should not use the principle of spiritual perfection in his work. Place in your own mind an idea of the particular character you wish to bring out and then know that the intelligence within you will give birth, through your imagination, to this idea.

THE OLD RUT

Question—Sometimes I catch a glimpse of truth and then I get back into the old rut, the old way of thinking, and a bunch of hard luck stares me in the face. How can I refuse to see limitations?

ANSWER—We do not always see the Truth clearly, but I should advise using the vision of your highest moments of thought as a pattern after which to work. Take the best your thought provides and repeatedly reaffirm it to be the truth about yourself, not fighting the images of limitation but, as it were, gently pushing them aside mentally and reaffirming your position in the Divine Mind as being one of unity with good. Know that the Truth is not bound by any existing conditions, that the higher law governs the lower, and endeavor to see yourself as being surrounded by everything which makes life happy and worthwhile.

CONTROLLING PSYCHIC DISTURBANCES

Question—I have been unable to hold a job due to the fact that I seem impelled at times to leave unceremoniously. I seem to be forced to obey some voice within. It is as though there were a master directing me. The condition brings severe pains across my body. Can you suggest a remedy?

ANSWER—You are evidently functioning on the psychic plane, or the "plane of many minds." I advise you, for your peace of mind, resolutely to climb higher. You are the only master who has a moral right to direct your own actions. There is a center within you through which the true intuition or guidance works; this is the well you must seek to tap; this is the point you must keep in mind as you do your daily work.

The treatment for you to practice is somewhat as follows: "By this word, which I recognize to be Pure Spirit, I free myself forever from everything that is contrary to the God-intended man—*my real Self*—and I (naming yourself), am under the direct and holy guidance of Truth. Anything less than Pure Truth cannot touch me. I know myself to be led to my right position, because my word establishes me there now. This word acts itself out for me without hindrance or delay." *Daily believing and speaking the word is necessary.*

RECOGNIZING LOVED ONES

Question—What is your conception of the lives of loved ones after their passing from this earthly life? Do you believe a form is taken as in this life? If not, how will we recognize the ones whom we firmly believe we shall see again some time?

ANSWER—The poet said that "soul is form and doth the body make." If this is true, and we believe that it is—if it is the soul and not the body that is immortalized—then there is every reason to suppose that the soul will project a definite form upon whatever plane it may function. It is also but natural to suppose that the soul will continue to project a body made after the image of its own remembrance. Hence we shall see and be seen, know and be known, after the transition which we call death.

RECONCILIATION

Question—There is inharmony between a very dear friend of mine and me. It is mostly caused by jealousy and selfishness on my part, and partly because of stubborn and false pride on the part of my friend. Will you assist me in working to bring about a complete reconciliation and happiness for us both again?

ANSWER—Jealousy, selfishness, stubbornness and false pride are all one and the same thing, and this thing is the destroyer of your peace; whatever vitality this thing has is supplied through your own mental action. Turn squarely away from the consideration of these unlovely qualities, then "whatsoever things are lovely" in yourself and your friend, "think on *these* things." Such a realization will keep you in a high love vibration. All good in the universe responds to this vibration.

In treating say this truth: "I give my friend perfect freedom, even as I want freedom for myself. I love my friend, and this love wipes out all apparently opposing forces. Only love can obtain."

WHEN WRONGLY ACCUSED

Question—I have been wrongly accused. I wish to avoid all controversy as well as misunderstanding on the part of my superiors. My accuser refuses to listen to reason. Please help me to know that justice and equity still rule.

ANSWER—Though all the reasoning in the world seemed to be absent from a situation, still the spiritual force of right action would ultimately prevail. Hold your own sense of right and justice firm and steady, and never doubt for one second that your good is yours *now*. Cast the burden on your Indwelling Christ for adjustment, knowing that neither thing, belief nor circumstance can hinder or delay the happy adjustment.

Should it be that you are dismissed from this position, never waver in your knowing that right is already an accomplished fact and that it manifests for you in this particular case. Don't be over-anxious to explain. No ears are so deaf as those that will not hear. "Bide your time." Your opportunity will surely come, and you will find that difficulties have been ironed out, that justice and equity still rule.

CULTIVATING PERSONAL MAGNETISM

Question—Can personal magnetism be cultivated, and has it any relation to will power?

ANSWER—Magnetism is defined in our textbook, *The Science of Mind*, as "the result of an abundant vitality on the physical plane, of intellect and temperament on the mental plane, and of atmosphere or consciousness on the Spiritual plane." It is therefore a natural force on every plane. Personality is the use that we make of our individuality, and since individuality is that which we really are, personality is of necessity much greater than it seems to be. Behind it are tremendous possibilities, and few realize the power it wields. If, by personal magnetism, you mean personal attractiveness or charm, it can and should be cultivated—not by the use of the human will but by a definite realization that the God within you radiates Itself through you as peace and poise, enthusiasm and charm. Our only approach to the Infinite is through our own divine nature, and every attribute of God necessary for a powerful and dynamic personality is established within you now. Know this daily and keep the mind directed to a high point on the spiritual plane. The higher the spiritual consciousness, the more irresistible the personality.

SEEKING HAPPINESS

Question—I am a widow, living with my parents who are very kind to me. But I am unhappy. My mother's health is such that I seem to be needed to keep house, though I would like to be earning money. It doesn't seem right to be dependent upon my father, who is getting on in age. I think I'd be far happier in my own home again. I have a lovely friend, a doctor, who calls on me twice a week and telephones me every day, but never mentions marriage. How can I be happier?

ANSWER—Perhaps the thought that you are a widow makes you unhappy. Possibly you have allowed yourself to feel that you are lonely. There is but One Presence. Realize your friends in this Presence and they will appear in the flesh.

Agree with what you are doing, since you may be unconsciously combating your present condition. If you wish a companion in life speak to the great Principle of all that lives. Do not pick out any particular person, for this is hypnotic suggestion and must always be avoided. The Truth knows just whom you can make happy and who will make you happy. Let the Truth work for you.

INDEX

If you would like to learn about our other publications or any of the ideas discussed in this book, you are cordially invited to write the publishers. There is no obligation. You may use the card in the back of the book or, if it has been removed, write:

SCIENCE OF MIND PUBLICATIONS
Dept. QA
P. O. Box 75127
Los Angeles, CA 90075